THE IMPROVISATION OF MUSICAL DIALOGUE

A Phenomenology of Music

What takes place when a composer creates a piece of music? To what extent is a performer part of the creative process? Although the dominant paradigm for music making in our era has been that of creation and reproduction – in which composers are the true "creators" and performers primarily carry out their wishes – does that way of thinking reflect actual musical practice?

By way of a phenomenology of music making, Bruce Ellis Benson argues for the innovative thesis that composers, performers, and even listeners are more properly seen as "improvisers." Working between the disciplines of philosophy and musicology, as well as the traditions of analytic and continental philosophy, Benson offers a rich tapestry of theoretical discussion interwoven with a wide range of musical examples from classical music, jazz, and other genres. He demonstrates how improvisation (defined in a broad rather than narrow sense) is essential to the entire phenomenon of music making. From the perspective of this improvisatory view, he suggests that music making is actually the continual creation and recreation of music – a constant improvisation.

Succinct and lucid, not only will this important book be a provocative read for philosophers of art and musicologists, it should also appeal to general readers, especially those who compose and perform music.

Bruce Ellis Benson is Associate Professor of Philosophy at Wheaton College (Illinois).

THE IMPROVISATION OF MUSICAL DIALOGUE

A Phenomenology of Music

BRUCE ELLIS BENSON

Wheaton College

CAMBRIDGE UNIVERSITY PRESS

PUBLISHED BY THE PRESS SYNDICATE OF THE UNIVERSITY OF CAMBRIDGE
The Pitt Building, Trumpington Street, Cambridge, United Kingdom

CAMBRIDGE UNIVERSITY PRESS
The Edinburgh Building, Cambridge CB2 2RU, UK
40 West 20th Street, New York, NY 10011-4211, USA
477 Williamstown Road, Port Melbourne, VIC 3207, Australia
Ruiz de Alarcón 13, 28014 Madrid, Spain
Dock House, The Waterfront, Cape Town 8001, South Africa

http://www.cambridge.org

First published 2003

Printed in the United Kingdom at the University Press, Cambridge

Typeface ITC New Baskerville 10/14 pt.   *System* LATEX 2$_\varepsilon$ [TB]

A catalog record for this book is available from the British Library.

Library of Congress Cataloging in Publication Data

Benson, Bruce Ellis, 1960–
The improvisation of musical dialogue : a phenomenology of music /
Bruce Ellis Benson.
p. cm.
Includes bibliographical references (p.) and index.
Contents: Between composition and performance – Composing: from Ursprung to
Fassung letzter Hand – Performing: the improvisation of preservation – The Ergon
with Energeia – The ethics of musical dialogue.
ISBN 0-521-81093-0 – ISBN 0-521-00932-4 (pb.)
1. Music – Philosophy and aesthetics. 2. Improvisation (Music) I. Title.
ML3845 .B358 2003
781.4′3117–dc21   2002067419

ISBN 0 521 81093 0 hardback
ISBN 0 521 00932 4 paperback

In memoriam

Hans-Georg Gadamer

(1900–2002)

I write pieces that are like drawings in a crayon book and the musicians color them themselves.

— Carla Bley

Interpreting language means: understanding language; interpreting music means: making music.

— Theodor Adorno

[Music] needs to be constantly changed and cannot bear many repetitions without making us weary.

— Immanuel Kant

Contents

Preface

O N LEARNING THAT I WAS WORKING ON A PHENOMENOLOGY of music making, one philosopher commented to me that, although he was also a musician, he had never wanted to think philosophically about music. He was worried that it might diminish the pleasure he derived from playing and listening to music. Somehow it was impossible to miss the hint of a suggestion that I follow his example.

No doubt there *are* ways of thinking and writing about music that could have that effect. Sometimes it seems that philosophers have lost sight of the musical experience itself, so that music ends up being treated as an ontological puzzle. For instance, although Roman Ingarden in many ways comes close to capturing the musical experience, toward the end of his life he made the astonishing admission that the primary focus of his phenomenology of music had not really been that of understanding music at all. Or in his own words: "The specifically aesthetic questions were to me at that time of secondary importance."[1] Ingarden's real concern was instead with the issue of realism versus idealism – and the

---

[1] Quoted in Max Rieser, "Roman Ingarden and His Time," *Journal of Aesthetics and Art Criticism* 29 (1971) 443.

work of art was just a particularly useful test case. Precisely this focus may help explain why, even though Ingarden's *Ontology of the Work of Art* purports to be a *phenomenology* of art works (including not merely musical works but also paintings, architecture, and film) and thus presumably guided by what Edmund Husserl termed the "things themselves" [*die Sachen selbst*], his real concern is to show that musical works remain "untouched" by performances.

Given that the actual phenomenon of making music has sometimes played second fiddle in philosophical reflections on music, it is not surprising that musicians have often wondered how those reflections relate to music making. In contrast, my concern is explicitly with what composers, performers, and listeners *do*. I have been continually goaded by the question that a fellow musician often asked when I was improvising at the piano: "What are you *doing*?" While he was primarily referring to the harmonic and structural changes that I was making, his question left me wondering what musicians really do. I still do not have a complete answer to that question. And perhaps that is all for the best: for music making is a wonderfully complex activity that resists precise definition.

What *is* clear to me, though, is that the binary schema of "composing" and "performing," which goes along with the construal of music making as being primarily about the production and reproduction of musical works, doesn't describe very well what musicians actually do. In its place, I wish to suggest an improvisational model of music, one that depicts composers, performers, and listeners as partners in dialogue. From this perspective, music is a conversation in which no one partner has exclusive control. Of course, the binary schema of composition/performance always *has* allowed for a kind of dialogue – and astute composers, performers, and listeners would be quick to point that out. Yet, I think the dialogical character of music making is not particularly well described by that binary schema and, furthermore, that the binary schema has significantly inhibited genuine dialogue.

To make that case, though, I first need to provide a phenomenology of musical experience. Briefly put, phenomenology is the attempt to bring the phenomena to light and, on the basis of the phenomena themselves, to develop a *logos* – a structure or theory. Thus, the point of considering the activities of composition and performance in depth is to see how they actually function and – on that basis – to construct a theory. On Husserl's view, philosophers are all too often guilty of constructing their theories and then attempting to "bend" the phenomena to fit those theories. Of course, there is no ultimate escape from this problem. One can merely seek to minimize it, and starting from the phenomena at least helps.

In Chapter 1, I sketch the way in which we usually *think* about music making, in effect providing a phenomenology of music theory. Then, in Chapters 2 and 3, I turn to the practices of composing and performing. Whereas Chapter 2 focuses on the ways in which composing involves improvisation, Chapter 3 shows how that improvisation is continued by performers. What we call "classical music" undoubtedly best exemplifies the composition/performance schema. Thus, my strategy will be to show where – even in classical music – that schema proves inadequate. And, if it proves inadequate in classical music, the implication is that it will likely fare even worse in describing other sorts of music. In Chapter 4, I provide a kind of improvisatory conception of music, with reference to classical music, jazz, and other genres. Those who long for neatly tied theories will likely be disappointed with my view of music in which the lines between composition and performance are hardly "neat." But I think that "messiness" simply reflects actual musical practice. Finally, in Chapter 5, I turn to the question of responsibilities of those who take part in the musical dialogue. What does it mean to respect the musical other? And how can there be room for both respect for the other and creativity?

Although the goal of this text is to provide a phenomenology of musical activity, there are at least two issues that underlie much of the discussion. One is ontology, specifically the ontological status of musical works. Such is the primary concern, naturally, of Ingarden's *Ontology of the Work of Art,* although much of his discussion on music touches (by necessity) on aspects of performance. In the same way, conversely, much of what follows will necessarily concern the ontology of the musical work. A second issue is that of hermeneutics, usually defined as the interpretation of texts. As such, it would seem to be primarily – or even solely – a matter of musical performance. But, since I hope to make clear that music making is *fundamentally* improvisational (in the broad sense that I describe in Chapter 1), then hermeneutical issues will be central to the entire discussion. While the "hermeneutics of music" certainly includes questions of composers' intentions, I argue that it goes far beyond them.[2] As should become evident, even though I think the intentions of composers can be known (at least to some extent) and should be respected, composers are not the only participants in the musical dialogue who have intentions, nor do their intentions necessarily trump the intentions of all other participants. Moreover, there may be different ways of respecting those intentions.[3]

[2] An excellent discussion of "authorial intention" – representing various sides of the issue – can be found in *Intention and Interpretation,* ed. Gary Iseminger (Philadelphia: Temple University Press, 1992).

[3] There is, of course, a further issue that naturally arises in a phenomenology of music: what "content" does music communicate? Given the wealth of resources on the subject, I have chosen not to focus on what music conveys. Of course, because I assume that composers (as well as performers and listeners) have intentions that go beyond simply the mechanics of sound production, I will at points make reference to the musical content of particular pieces.

Preface

Both the ontological and hermeneutical aspects are central to Gadamer's thought. On Gadamer's account, musical performance has the same basic interpretational structure characteristic of reading a text or seeing a piece of visual art.[4] In other words, reading a text is in effect a "performance," *for only in reading does the text truly exist*. And I think Gadamer is right in insisting on this performance character of interpretation. Yet, although that structure is similar in crucial ways, there is an important difference. For, while reading a text or encountering a piece of visual art is something that can be done silently, the result of a performance must be that of *sound*. There can be no silent musical performance. As Adorno puts it, "interpreting language means: understanding language; interpreting music means: making music."[5]

Making music is what this book is all about. While writing on music could have the effect of spoiling the musical experience, my hope is to do precisely the opposite.

It goes without saying that my work would not be possible were it not for the work of many others. Yet, since my way of thinking about music making heavily emphasizes the role of the other, acknowledging that dependence is particularly appropriate, and I do so gladly. My thanks to Elizabeth A. Behnke, Rudolf Bernet, Hermann Danuser, William Desmond, Garry Hagberg, Otto Pöggeler, Gunther Scholz, F. Joseph Smith, Bernhard Waldenfels, and Merold Westphal, all of whom not only provided insight but encouragement. Thanks also to Carla Bley, who allowed me to include her words in the epigraph. And thanks to Wilfried Joris for asking.

4 Hans-Georg Gadamer, *Truth and Method*, 2nd rev. ed., rev. trans. Joel Weinsheimer and Donald G. Marshall (New York: Crossroad, 1989) xxxi.
5 Theodor W. Adorno, "Fragment über Musik und Sprache," in *Sprache, Dictung, Musik*, ed. Jakob Knaus (Tübingen: Max Niemeyer, 1973) 73.

Preface

I am grateful to Hans-Georg Gadamer, who graciously encouraged me at the beginning of the project and subsequently was willing to read and critique an early part of it. Those familiar with his thought will no doubt see how much I am indebted to him. Gadamer had long hoped to see his hermeneutics applied to music. I am only sorry that he did not live to see this book's completion.

My research would have been impossible without the generous financial assistance of the Belgian-American Education Foundation, the Fulbright Commission, the *Onderzoeksfonds* of the University of Leuven, and the Wheaton College Alumni Association.

Finally, I would be greatly amiss were I not to recognize the support that I have received for this project – all along the way – from my mother and late father and a cadre of friends and musicians too numerous to mention here. To Jackie, thanks for appreciating my own music making, and everything else.

ONE

Between Composition and Performance

Suppose that someone has improvised on the organ. And suppose that he then goes home and scores a work of such a sort that his improvisation, judged by the requirements for correctness specified in the score, is at all points correct. In spite of that, the composer did not compose his work *in* performing his improvisation. In all likelihood, he did not even compose it *while* improvising. For in all likelihood he did not, during his improvising, finish selecting that particular set of requirements for correctness of occurrence to be found in the score.[1]

So at what point *is* a composer finished? If a musical work does not (quite) exist while it is being improvised, what further steps are required to bring it into being and to solidify and define its being so that it may be pronounced "done?" Moreover, assuming that Wolterstorff is right in maintaining that composing is the act of *selecting* the properties that are to form the work, how does such selection take place and when does that decision process come to an end? Furthermore, what exactly is the line

---

[1] Nicholas Wolterstorff, *Works and Worlds of Art* (Oxford: Clarendon Press, 1980) 64.

that separates composing and performing? Is there a clear line of demarcation, or are what we call "composing" and "performing" better understood as two facets of one activity? And, if performing is to be defined in terms of following the rules of correctness that the composer has set down, what does it mean to follow those rules? In other words, what exactly counts as *essential* to a piece of music's identity (and thus necessary to a "correct" performance of it), as opposed to something that is merely open to the performer's discretion?

The question of *when* a piece of music can be rightly said to exist depends heavily upon how we construe the activities known as composing and performing. If composing is a process, we need to examine what delimits that process, at either end. Is the composer the sole creator of a musical work, in the sense of initiating and terminating the process of composition? Or is the composing process rather something that extends beyond the composer – perhaps in both directions – with the result that the composer is *also* merely a participant in a particular musical discourse or practice?

Contrary to Wolterstorff's claim that "to improvise is not to compose,"[2] I will argue that the process by which a work comes into existence is *best* described as improvisatory at its very core, not merely the act of composing but also the acts of performing and listening. On my view, improvisation is not something that *precedes* composition (*pace* Wolterstorff) or stands outside and opposed to composition. Instead, I think that the activities that we call "composing" and "performing" are essentially improvisational in nature, even though improvisation takes many different forms in each activity. As we shall see, if my claim is correct, the beginnings and endings of musical pieces may indeed be "real" (as opposed to merely "imagined"), but they are often messy.

[2] Ibid.

Exactly where and when they begin and end may not be easy to specify.

Composition, Works, and Performance

The claim that music is fundamentally improvisatory is hardly intuitively obvious. Rather, it may well seem simply untrue. But I think that the reason we are reluctant to accept such a characterization stems more from the way in which we happen to think about music than from actual musical practice. Briefly put, we tend to assume that music making is primarily about the creation and preservation of musical works. And the reason we think that way is because the dominant form of music – or at least the form that has been the basis for most theoretical reflection – is that of "classical music."[3] The hegemony of classical music has had significant results in shaping musical theory. One can easily argue, for instance, that its dominance has led theorists to overlook important differences between various sorts of music. Yet, such theoretical reflection has done a significant injustice even to classical music itself, for it distorts the actual practice of music making in classical music *itself*.

For the moment, though, we need to consider exactly how our thinking about music is shaped. While there are various factors that define the practice known as classical music, I think there are two basic concepts or ideals that are particularly prominent in that practice, and thus in our thinking. They are (1) the ideal of *Werktreue* and (2) the ideal of composer as "true creator." Far from being unique to my study, these two concepts have been

---

[3] Unless otherwise indicated, I will use the term "classical music" to denote the sort of music performed in a concert hall (i.e., classical music in a broad sense), rather than merely music that comes after "Baroque" and before "Romantic" (Classical music with a capital "C").

discussed by musicologists such as Carl Dahlhaus and philosophers such as Lydia Goehr, who has provided not only a
description of the way in which the concept of the musical work
has shaped the practice of classical music but also an insightful
genealogy of the work concept.[4] But, whereas the purpose of
Dahlhaus and Goehr is to provide an explanation of how these
ideals have functioned in ordering the practice of classical music,
I will sketch these ideals in this chapter with the ultimate purpose
of providing an alternative.

As an illustration of what the ideal of *Werktreue* is *not*, consider
the following piece of advice, given to performers in the early
eighteenth century:

> The manner in which all *Airs* divided into three Parts [*da capo*
> arias] are to be sung. In the first they require nothing but the
> simplest Ornaments, of a good Taste and few, that the Compo-
> sition may remain simple, plain and pure; in the second they
> expect, that to this Purity some artful Graces be added, by which
> the Judicious may hear, that the Ability of the Singer is greater;
> and in repeating the *Air*, he that does not vary it for the better,
> is no master.[5]

Contemporary performers are apt to be uncomfortable following such advice. The ritual of performance in classical music is
highly regulated and a crucial part of that ritual is that such advice
is inappropriate. Of course, it once *was* deemed appropriate, in

---

4 See particularly Carl Dahlhaus, *Nineteenth-Century Music*, trans. J. Bradford
  Robinson (Berkeley and Los Angeles: University of California Press,
  1989) and Lydia Goehr, *The Imaginary Museum of Musical Works* (Oxford:
  Clarendon Press, 1992). The view that I sketch in this chapter is roughly
  what Stan Godlovitch would term the "subordination view." See his *Musical
  Performance: A Philosophical Study* (London: Routledge, 1998) 81–4.
5 Pier Francesco Tosi, *Opinioni de'cantori antichi, e moderni* (Bologna, 1723);
  Observations on the Florid Song, trans. J. E. Galliard (London, 1724)
  93. Quoted in Robert Donington, *Baroque Music: Style and Performance*
  (London: Faber Music, 1982) 95.

Tosi's day; but such improvisation would be highly questionable to performers today. In contrast, our conception of the role of a classical musician is far closer to that of self-effacing servant who faithfully serves the score of the composer. Admittedly, performers are given a certain degree of leeway; but the unwritten rules of the game are such that this leeway is relatively small and must be kept in careful check.

The idea(1) of being "*treu*" – which can be translated as "true" or "faithful" – implies faithfulness to someone or something. *Werktreue*, then, is directly a kind of faithfulness to the *Werk* (work) and, indirectly, a faithfulness to the composer. Given the centrality of musical notation in the discourse of classical music, a parallel notion is that of *Texttreue*: fidelity to the written score. Indeed, we can say that *Werktreue* has normally been thought to entail *Texttreue*. Not only does the ideal of *Werktreue* say a great deal about our expectations of performers, it also implies a very particular way of thinking about music: one in which the work of music has a prominent place. The idea of the musical work clearly controls the way we (that is, those of us in Western culture) think about not only classical music but simply music in general. Jan L. Broeckx goes so far as to say that "for some centuries, western theorists of music have identified the concept of "music" with the totality of all actual and conceivable musical works – and with nothing but that."[6] It is not surprising, then, that Jerrold Levinson claims that musical works are "the center and aim of the whole enterprise" of musical activity.[7]

Assuming, for the moment, that the activity of making music can be adequately described in terms of the creation and reproduction of musical works, what exactly is a work of music? Or

[6] Jan L. Broeckx, *Contemporary Views on Musical Style and Aesthetics* (Antwerp: Metropolis, 1979) 126.
[7] Jerrold Levinson, "What a Musical Work Is," in *Music, Art, and Metaphysics* (Ithaca, N.Y.: Cornell University Press, 1990) 67.

perhaps we should instead ask: what exactly do we *think* we are talking about when we speak of a work of music? Goehr rightly points out that there have been various sorts of philosophical theories of musical works and they can be differentiated as Platonist, modified Platonist, Aristotelian, and so on.[8] But my concern here is less with their differences than with their fundamental commonalities: for what these views have in common is the assumption that musical works have an essentially *ideal* quality, particularly in terms of their *identity*. And these theories have not affected merely the theorists. Thus, we usually assume that pieces of music are discrete, autonomous entities that stand on their own, a view that is intimately linked with our conception of art works in general.

While there are many ways of explaining this ideal character of musical works, the schema that Husserl sets up is remarkably similar to most accounts, at least in its primary features. Key to Husserl's conception of ideal objects is that they are essentially *spiritual* entities that have an ideal rather than real existence.[9] Although this certainly could be taken in a Platonic sense, Husserl (at least in later works) does not have Platonic ideals in mind. For ideal objects of the Husserlian variety exist neither in some Platonic realm nor eternally; rather, they are part of what Husserl terms the "cultural world" and are created (rather than discovered) by human activity. However, whereas real objects have an existence in space and time, ideal objects do not. Instead, they have a timeless existence (i.e., once they are created) that can be characterized as "omnitemporal," for they are "everywhere and nowhere" and so "can appear simultaneously in many spatiotemporal positions and yet be numerically identical as the

---

[8] See *The Imaginary Museum of Musical Works* 13ff.

[9] Also see Alfred Schutz, "Fragments on the Phenomenology of Music," in *In Search of Musical Method*, ed. F. Joseph Smith (New York: Gordon and Breach, 1976) 27ff.

same."[10] It is this ability to be endlessly repeated and still retain their identity that marks ideal objects as unique. For Husserl, plays, novels, concepts, and musical works all have this ability. Moreover, what makes them ideal in another sense is that – in virtue of having an existence disconnected from the world of real objects – they would seem to be protected from the caprices of the real world and thus the dangers that threaten the existence of real objects.

Yet, in what sense is, say, a symphony of Bruckner not a real object? What could be more real than the sounds heard or the score from which the musicians play? Husserl does not mean to imply that musical sounds or notations are not real; instead, he intends to distinguish between a particular performance (or instantiation) and the ideal entity itself. "However much [the *Kreutzer Sonata*] consists of sounds, it is an ideal unity; and its constituent sounds are no less ideal."[11] What Husserl means is that, whereas a *performance* of the *Kreutzer Sonata* consists of real sounds, a performance is merely a physical embodiment of the ideal entity. Thus, although "Goethe's *Faust* is found in any number of real books," these are simply "exemplars of *Faust*," not *Faust* itself.[12] The "real" *Faust* is not the *Faust* of the real world. Naturally, Husserl realizes that even ideal objects can have strong or relatively weak connections to the real world. What he calls *free idealities* (for example, geometric theorems) have little connection to any particular historical or cultural context. One doesn't, for instance, need to know much about the early Greeks to be able to understand the Pythagorean Theorem; one only needs to

[10] Edmund Husserl, *Experience and Judgment: Investigations in a Genealogy of Logic*, trans. James S. Churchill and Karl Ameriks, ed. Ludwig Landgrebe (Evanston, Ill.: Northwestern University Press, 1973) 260–1.
[11] Edmund Husserl, *Formal and Transcendental Logic*, trans. Dorion Cairns (The Hague: Martinus Nijhoff, 1978) 21.
[12] *Experience and Judgment* 266.

understand basic geometry. *Bound idealities*, on the other hand, are those having a particular place in cultural history, such as novels or musical works.

Something like Husserl's distinction is found in everyday language. We often speak of performing and practicing a piece of music as if that piece were distinct from the performances and practicing of them. Moreover, Husserl's theory of ideal objects is hardly unique: for the model that it employs – that of an ideal something that has material embodiments – is similar to C. S. Peirce's distinction between type and token, ideal objects being types and the material instantiations of ideal objects their tokens. Many philosophers have defined musical works in terms of the type/token model. For instance, Richard Wollheim claims that "*Ulysses* and *Der Rosenkavalier* are types, my copy of *Ulysses* and tonight's performance of *Der Rosenkavalier* are tokens of those types."[13]

There are certain basic assumptions about the work that stand behind this model, and these govern the practice of classical music. First, it is not insignificant that Wolterstorff defines composing as an activity in which "the composer selects properties of sounds *for the purpose of their serving as criteria for judging correctness of occurence.*"[14] Composers set up boundaries both to define the work *and* to restrict the activity of the performer. Accordingly, Wolterstorff considers a musical work to be a "norm-kind," in the sense of setting up a norm that the performer is to follow. Similarly, although Nelson Goodman takes a nominalistic view of the work (for he claims that there is no type, just tokens), the ideal of compliance is foremost: he maintains that "complete compliance with the score is the only requirement for a genuine instance of a

[13] See Charles Sanders Peirce, *Collected Papers*, Vol. IV (Cambridge, Mass.: Harvard University Press, 1939) no. 537 and Richard Wollheim, *Art and Its Objects*, 2nd ed. (Cambridge: Cambridge University Press, 1980) 65.
[14] *Works and Worlds of Art* 62 (my italics).

work" and this compliance is "categorically required." Thus, "the most miserable performance without actual mistakes does count as such an instance, while the most brilliant performance with a single wrong note does not."[15] While Wolterstorff and Goodman place particular emphasis on the limitations that a work sets on performers, such an emphasis is not peculiar to their theories. Rather, it reflects the ideals of the practice known as classical music.

Second, a different though clearly related emphasis is on preservation. Goodman claims that "work-preservation is paramount" and this leads him to argue that "if we allow the least deviation [from the score], all assurance of work-preservation and score-preservation is lost."[16] It is hardly surprising, then, that creativity in performance not only has no importance in his theory but would be viewed as inappropriate. While Goodman's theory is somewhat extreme (both in this respect and others), he is clearly reflecting an important assumption: we tend to see both the score and the performance primarily as vehicles for *preserving* what the composer has created. We assume that musical scores provide a permanent record or embodiment in signs; in effect, a score serves to "fix" or objectify a musical work. Likewise, although we *do* expect performances to be creative in some limited sense, we see them *primarily* as part of a preservational chain.

Not only does this concept of the work define for us what music is but, more important, it provides a model for thinking about what is involved in music making. According to this model, composers create musical works and performers reproduce them. That is hardly to say that performance is exclusively reproductive in nature (for clearly the performer adds *something*

---

[15] Nelson Goodman, *Languages of Art: An Approach to a Theory of Symbols* (Indianapolis: Bobbs-Merrill, 1968) 186–7.

[16] Ibid. 178 and 186–7.

in the process of performance). Yet, it seems safe to say that performance is – on this paradigm – primarily reproductive and only secondarily creative. Nothing illustrates the model of composition and performance that dominates the practice of classical music better than the title of the book on performance by Hans Pfitzner (who, incidentally, happened to be a composer): *Werk und Wiedergabe* – which can be translated as "work and reproduction."[17] Given this model, it is understandable that we make a definite distinction not only between performance and improvisation but also between works and transcriptions or arrangements. We assume that a musical work has a well-defined identity, so transcriptions (which are often revisions of the work to make it playable for another instrument) and arrangements (which tend to be more significant in their "revising" of the work, in order to make a piece more suitable for a different context or else provide a different listening experience) are usually seen as separate ontological entities.

Behind this notion of the work and faithfulness to it is our second ideal, that the composer is the true creator in the activity of music making. Levinson provides a perfect expression of this viewpoint:

> There is probably no idea more central to thought about art than . . . that it is a godlike activity in which the artist brings into being what did not exist beforehand – much as a demiurge forms a world out of inchoate matter. . . . There is a special aura that envelops composers, as well as other artists, because we think of them as true creators.[18]

Despite the fact that Bach insisted that anyone could have done what he did with enough hard work, the way we conceive of the composing process minimizes the influence of tradition (not to

---

[17] Hans Pfitzner, *Werk und Wiedergabe* (Augsburg: Benno Filsner, 1929).
[18] "What a Musical Work Is" 66–7.

mention the role of effort) and instead emphasizes the special "powers" of the individual composer. Given this conception of composer as demiurge, it is not surprising that composition tends to be seen as a mysterious process. And the assumption that the composer is a true creator has proven decisive in regulating the practice of classical music. Perhaps the single most important influence has to do with the composer's intentions and how we are to handle them. The musicologist Donald Jay Grout begins an essay on performance by, as he puts it, "setting down some truisms," the first of which is that "an ideal performance is one that perfectly realizes the composer's intentions."[19] A great deal of the importance that we ascribe to performers is actually a kind of derivative importance: in effect, they are like priests whose prestige comes primarily from being mediators between listeners and the great composers.

While this characterization might be criticized as somewhat extreme, it reflects the thinking of at least *many* composers *and* performers in the past two centuries. Whereas Haydn claimed that "the free arts and the so beautiful science of composition tolerate no shackling" (an understandable sentiment from some- one forced to wear the livery while in the service of Prince Esterházy), Carl Maria von Weber went so far as to demand that the composer become "free as a god."[20] In light of this conception of the composer as god or demiurge, E. T. A. Hoffmann (writing in a review of Beethoven's Fifth Symphony) provides the following guideline for the performer: "The true

---

[19] Donald Jay Grout, "On Historical Authenticity in the Performance of Old Music," in *Essays in Honor of Archibald Thompson Davison* (Cambridge, Mass.: Harvard University Press, 1957) 341.

[20] Friedrich Blume, *Classic and Romantic Music: A Comprehensive Survey*, trans. M. D. Herter Norton (New York: Norton, 1970) 91 and Walter Salmen, "Social Obligations of the Emancipated Musician in the 19th Century," in *The Social Status of the Professional Musician from the Middle Ages to the 19th Century*, ed. Walter Salmen (New York: Pendragon, 1983) 270.

artist lives only in the work that he conceives and then performs as the composer intended it. He disdains to let his own personality intervene in any way."[21]

By the twentieth century, this way of thinking about the respective roles of composer and performer had become more or less the norm. For example, Paul Hindemith speaks of the performer as "the intermediate transformer station," whose role is to "duplicate the preëstablished values of the composer's creation."[22] Aaron Copland likewise characterizes the performer as "a kind of middleman" who "exists to serve the composer."[23] An even more striking example of the view that performers ought to know their place (and stay there) is that of Igor Stravinsky, who sees the role of the performer as "the strict putting into effect of an explicit will [i.e., the composer's will] that contains nothing beyond what it specifically commands."[24] Stravinsky attempts to beat performers back into cowering "submission" (to use his term). He rails vehemently against "sins" against either the "letter" or "spirit" of a composition, "criminal assaults" against the composer's text, and "betraying" the composer (who, in turn, becomes a "victim"). What he demands is "the conformity

---

[21] *E. T. A. Hoffmann's Musical Writings:* Kreisleriana, The Poet and the Composer, *Music Criticism,* ed. David Charlton, trans. Martyn Clarke (Cambridge: Cambridge University Press, 1989) 103.

[22] Paul Hindemith, *A Composer's World: Horizons and Limitations* (Garden City, N.Y.: Anchor, 1961) 153.

[23] Aaron Copland, *What to Listen for in Music* (New York: McGraw-Hill, 1957) 258. Elsewhere, Copland does recognize that "every performance that has been logically conceived represents a reading in some sense." See *Music and Imagination* (Cambridge, Mass.: Harvard University Press, 1952) 53.

[24] Igor Stravinsky, *Poetics of Music,* trans. Arthur Knoedel and Ingolf Dahl (New York: Vintage, 1947) 127. It was Richard Taruskin's account of Stravinsky that first made me aware of Stravinsky's "quasi-religious fundamentalism" (as Taruskin so aptly puts it). See his "The Pastness of the Present and the Presence of the Past" in Richard Taruskin, *Text and Act: Essays on Music and Performance* (New York: Oxford University Press, 1995) 129.

of that presentation to the composer's will." It is clear who is supposed to be in charge.[25]

Given the kinds of expectations of composers such as Hindemith, Copland, and Stravinsky, it is not surprising that Ingarden – in giving what he takes to be merely a phenomenological description of the musical work – speaks of the notes of the score as "*imperative symbols*."[26] In effect, they have a *moral* force, in the sense that the performer is supposed to *obey* them. Similarly, I take it that Wolterstorff and Goodman are simply expressing the dominant view of the "moral" force that scores carry.

It is no mere coincidence that the views expressed by Hindemith, Copland, and Stravinsky sound so remarkably similar: twentieth-century composers have been among the most ardent proponents of the view of performer as "mouthpiece" of the composer rather than as "co-creator." This is not to say that performers are superfluous, since, at least in most cases, composers need performers to present their works to their listeners. To at least that extent, then, performers are vital. Moreover, whether composers like it or not, listeners often expect performances to exhibit a certain level of creativity. Of course, that expectation doesn't always fit very well with the expectation of fidelity. But, as with many things, our expectations are often contradictory. Still, it seems fair to say that we (and that "we" includes composers, performers, and listeners alike) tend to view the role of the performer more as middleman than as co-creator.

The idea that the performer is almost a "necessary evil" has sometimes even been carried over to the listener. Regarding what he terms "consideration for the listener," Schoenberg writes in a letter: "I have as little of this as he has for me. I only know

---

[25] *Poetics of Music* 129–30 and 139.
[26] Roman Ingarden, *Ontology of the Work of Art: The Musical Work – The Picture – The Architectural Work – The Film,* trans. Raymond Meyer with John T. Goldthwait (Athens: Ohio University Press, 1989) 25 (my italics).

that he exists, and as long as he is not indispensable on acoustic grounds (since music does not sound right in an empty hall), he annoys me."[27] For Schoenberg, then, listeners become merely an acoustic necessity – and an annoying one at that.

The ideal of *Werktreue* has proven so hegemonic that it has even spilled over from classical music into other genres. For instance, in the last decade, both Wynton Marsalis (with the Lincoln Center Jazz Orchestra) and William Russo (with the Chicago Jazz Ensemble) have provided us with painstakingly historically accurate performances of Duke Ellington compositions – along with Ellingtonian performance practice. One can easily argue that Ellington's compositions are as worthy of preservation as those composing the classical canon. But Marsalis's performance practice seems to go against his earlier stated views on the difference between classical music and jazz. As he puts it: "Concert musicians are artisans – Jazz musicians are artists." Parsing out that distinction, jazz musicians have in effect the role of creator similar to that of classical composers. Thus, with this distinction in mind, Marsalis insists that – in performing classical music (and Marsalis certainly speaks as an accomplished performer of classical music) – "the best thing you can do is not mess it up."[28] Yet, in seeking an historically accurate performance of jazz, Marsalis's goal is no longer that of "improvisation" but simply "not messing it up." Understandably, Marsalis has been criticized by some as promoting a conception of jazz that turns it into a "museum."

Clearly, any musical practice that has the notions of *Werktreue* and the composer as "true" creator as its ideals – whether that be classical music or jazz or any other genre – cannot help but end up tending in the direction of a kind of monologue in which

[27] Arnold Schoenberg, *Ausgewählte Briefe*, ed. Erwin Stein (Mainz: B. Schott's Soehne, 1958) 52.
[28] See Marsalis's remarks in Bruce Buschel, "Angry Young Man with a Horn," *Gentlemen's Quarterly* (February 1987) 195.

the principal voice is that of the composer. But such a model represents only *one* way of thinking about music. What other possibilities might there be?

Beethoven or Rossini?

Gadamer claims that an ideal dialogue has what he calls the "*logical structure of openness.*" I think there are at least two aspects to this "openness." First, the conversation often brings something into the open: it sheds new light on what is being discussed and allows us to think about it (or, in this case, *hear* it) in a new way. Second, the dialogue is itself open, since it (to quote Gadamer) is in a "state of indeterminacy."[29] In order for a genuine dialogue to take place, the outcome cannot be settled in advance. Without at least some "loose-play" or uncertainty, true conversation is impossible. But, of course, this is an ideal for conversations, not necessarily a reflection of how they always operate. Moreover, Gadamer recognizes that those participating in a dialogue usually have certain expectations of how it should function. In saying that genuine dialogues are characterized by "openness," Gadamer hardly means to suggest that dialogues ought to have no rules. Precisely the rules are what allow the conversation to take place at all. In effect, they open up a kind of space in which dialogue can be conducted.[30] Yet, even though rules are clearly necessary for a dialogue even to exist, those rules can be restrictive or comparatively open. Open dialogues are governed by rules that are flexible – and are themselves open to continuing modification.

It hardly needs to be said that, viewed as a dialogue, the practice of classical music is not particularly open. Historically, though, our current way of thinking about music has hardly been the

[29] *Truth and Method* 362–3.
[30] Ibid. 107.

only option. Indeed, it is a way of thinking that is – at least to a great extent – remarkably *recent*. So what are the alternatives? Are we faced with a choice between *Werktreue* and no guidelines at all (so that "anything goes")? It is far too simplistic merely to give up the ideal of *Werktreue*: we need something in its place. Instead of looking forward for a different model to guide our music making, I suggest that we look back. For, although the ideals of the discourse of classical music have so dominated our thought for the past two centuries that it seems difficult even to imagine another way of thinking about music, note that in the early 1800s this way of thinking represented merely *a* model of music rather than *the* model. What characterized that age were two very different ways of thinking about music making – that of Beethoven and that of Rossini. And it was clearly Beethoven who was the innovator.

Although we might be tempted to think of Beethoven and Rossini as merely representing two different musical styles, that difference is clearly *philosophical* in nature: for at stake are two different ways of *conceiving* not only the nature of musical works and the role of the performance in presenting them but also the connection between the artist and the community. On the one hand, Beethoven saw his symphonies as "inviolable musical 'texts' whose meaning is to be deciphered with 'exegetical' interpretations; a Rossini score, on the other hand, is a mere recipe for a performance."[31] What accounts for this difference is that Rossini thought of his music not as a "work" but as something that came into existence only in the moment of performance. In practice, this meant that a piece of music had no fixed identity and so could be adapted for a given performance. Thus, the performer had an important a role in the creation of musical works. Even more important, it was not the *work* that was given

[31] *Nineteenth-Century Music* 9.

precedence; rather, the work (and thus the composer) was in effect a partner in dialogue with performers and listeners.

Interestingly enough, in his lectures on aesthetics, Hegel makes a distinction between two kinds of performers that clearly reflects the influence of these two different musical models. On the one hand, the first sort of performer "does not wish to render anything beyond what the work in hand already contains." Indeed "the executant artist not only need not, but must not, add anything of his own, or otherwise he will spoil the effect. He must submit himself entirely to the character of the work and intend to be only an obedient instrument." Here we have a statement of the ideal of *Werktreue* that is as forceful and as uncompromising as any. On the other hand, Hegel's second version of the performer (and he explicitly mentions Rossini in this regard) is of one who "composes in his interpretation, fills in what is missing, deepens what is superficial, ensouls what is soulless and in this way appears as plainly independent and productive. So, for example, in Italian opera much is always left to the singer: particularly in embellishment he is left room for free play." As a result, *"we have present before us not merely a work of art but the actual production of one."*[32] In music making of this sort, the performer and the composer work together as co-creators, thus blurring the line between the composer and the performer.

Of course, one might be tempted to counter at this point that Beethoven's texts just *are* such that they call for an "executant artist," whereas Rossini's scores call for what we might term an "embellishing artist." Such an argument might take the form: "If we examine a Beethoven score, we realize that it has

---

[32] Georg Wilhelm Friedrich Hegel, *Aesthetics: Lectures on Fine Art*, Vol. II, trans. T. M. Knox (Oxford: Oxford University Press, 1975) 955–7 (my italics; translation modified).

more requirements than one of Rossini. Therefore, performers of Beethoven's music are necessarily executant artists." But simply appealing to the score and its requirements doesn't necessarily establish that performers of Beethoven either *are* or *must be* "executant artists." Do Beethoven scores leave room for the performer to act as "co-creator?" That depends on how we construe what the performer *does* in performing them. Furthermore, to what extent is the performer *obligated* to reproduce the expectations of the composer? Merely because Beethoven had stricter expectations for his performers than did Rossini does not automatically place stricter obligations on performers of his music. These are questions to which we will return.

In any case, whereas what we might term "Beethoven's view" results in musical activity that tends toward a monologue, "Rossini's view" allows much more possibility for a genuine dialogue in which composers, performers, and listeners are co-creators. On my read, Rossini's view offers a better conception of musical community. More than this, I will argue in subsequent chapters that it likewise better describes actual musical practice – even for music by, say, Beethoven. For, as Hegel goes on to say in describing the role of the executant performer, if "art is still to be in question, the artist (*Künstler*) has the duty of giving life and soul to the work in the same sense as the composer did, and not to give the impression of being a musical automaton who recites a mere lesson and repeats mechanically what has been dictated to him."[33] So, according to Hegel, even the "executant" artist ought to be more than simply a "middleman." And I think that is both what we *want* performers to do and also what they *actually do*.

Thus, there is a clear precedent for thinking about music as an open sort of dialogue. And it doesn't begin merely with Rossini. What we know about the performance practice of Renaissance

[33] Ibid. 956.

and Baroque music makes it clear that performance in those eras was heavily improvisational – and composers expected as much. David Fuller characterizes Baroque music as follows: "a large part of the music of the whole era was sketched rather than fully realized, and the performer had something of the responsibility of a child with a coloring book, to turn these sketches into rounded art-works." Baroque music functioned somewhat analogously to that of jazz today, so that a jazz "fake book" (in which only the melody and chords are notated and the musician "fakes" the rest) is not so unlike the scores used by Baroque musicians. Essentially, then, Baroque performances were constantly in flux, so that they varied (as Fuller puts it) "from one group to the next, one day to the next, one neighbourhood to the next." In 1549, Bermudo described the situation by saying "the fashion of playing them changes every day."[34]

The very idea that performers were essentially expected to *reproduce* what was in the score was a foreign notion, for the idea of musical works – as completed and carefully delimited entities – did not exist. To take a concrete example: the very idea of a "correct" performance of Handel's *Messiah* turns out to be highly problematic, for Handel himself never provided anything like a definitive version of *Messiah*. Instead, all we have are competing versions in which Handel constantly changes all sorts of things to fit the many occasions on which it was performed.[35] If we take Handel's operas as an example, what we have are compositions that "are neither 'all of a piece' nor unalterable but can always be reshaped – at least by Handel himself – as though they were

---

[34] David Fuller, "The Performer as Composer," in *Performance Practice*, Vol. II, ed. Howard Mayer Brown and Stanley Sadie (Houndmills, U.K.: Macmillan, 1989) 117–18.

[35] See Watkins Shaw, *A Textual and Historical Companion to Handel's* Messiah (London: Novello, 1965), Chapter 5.

living organisms."[36] There was no conception of there being a "work" with a fully stable identity.[37]

This flexibility meant that performers and composers were seen as engaged in tasks that were not nearly so strongly and neatly defined as our conceptions of "composer" and "performer" today. The assumption was that performers were to contribute their fair share to the creation of a musical composition. There were, of course, those who complained about excessive extemporization and some composers, such as J. S. Bach and Couperin, went so far as to write out embellishments to their pieces. Couperin protested vehemently when these were not followed: "I am always astonished ... to hear persons who have learnt my pieces without heeding my instructions. Such negligence is unpardonable.... I therefore declare that my pieces must be performed just as I have written them."[38] Yet, Couperin's perception that there was a need to put a curb on embellishing tells us a great deal about actual musical practice of the time, as well as the fact that Bach was soundly criticized for writing everything out. Even Handel's outburst during a rehearsal – "You toc! Don't I know better as your seluf, vaat is pest for you to sing!"[39] – serves to give us an idea of just how "seriously" singers took Handel's own direction (as well as just how far he was willing

[36] Reinhard Strohm, *Essays on Handel and Italian Opera* (Cambridge: Cambridge University Press, 1985) 102.

[37] Although Nicolai Listenius is sometimes mentioned as the originator of the idea of the musical work (c. 1527 or 1537), his conception of the work differs from our modern one; and musical practice of the time was certainly not regulated by this ideal. See the discussions in Wilhelm Seidel, *Werk und Werkbegriff in der Musikgeschichte* (Darmstadt: Wissenschaftliche Buchgesellschaft, 1987) 3-8 and *The Imaginary Museum of Musical Works* 115-18.

[38] From the preface to *Pièces de clavecin: Troisième livre* (Paris, 1722), quoted in Peter Le Huray, *Authenticity in Performance: Eighteenth-Century Case Studies* (Cambridge: Cambridge University Press, 1990) 59.

[39] I am indebted to an anonymous reader from Cambridge for this quote.

to let the dialogue go). So, like any dialogue, not just *anything* was acceptable. There were still rules. But, having said that, it is clear that performers were expected to be much more active improvisers than in the dialogue of classical music of today. G. C. Weitzler, for instance, insisted that "a musical person with good interpretive powers will never play in the same way but will always make modifications [i.e., in the notes] in accordance with the state of his feelings."[40] Rather than being some sort of strange deviation in the history of performance practice, Weitzler and Tosi (quoted earlier in this chapter) express what would have been more or less the norm.

Not only was music constantly in flux, but precisely the fact that it was designed primarily to serve a particular function meant that the idea of composing a work that was expected to continue to exist beyond the life of the composer was simply not a guiding ideal of musical composition. Thus, performances were generally of music written by contemporaries; indeed, the performer in many cases was the composer. As a result, musical compositions were generally remarkably short lived. Writing in the fifteenth century, for instance, Johannes Tinctoris made what might seem to us to be an audacious claim – that compositions older than forty years simply were not worth listening to. Of course, an important factor for Tinctoris's seeming musical snobbery was simply the way composers earned their livelihoods: many composers were in the service either of the church or of a patron, both of which meant that they were under pressure to come up with new works on a regular basis. During the time J. S. Bach served as the cantor at the Thomaskirche in Leipzig, it was simply expected that he have something new for the choir to sing on

[40] Marpurg, *Historisch-Kritische Beyträge* III (Berlin, 1756), quoted in Robert Donington, *The Interpretation of Early Music*, new rev. ed. (London: Faber and Faber, 1989) 157.

Sundays and church holidays. And this was equally the case for secular performances: the life of an Italian opera was usually no more than ten years.[41] Composers did not view their compositions as something designed to last for eternity but as something to be performed during their lifetime. Naturally, this had important implications for performance practice: since composers were continually expected to create something new, performers were usually engaged in performing new works rather than old ones. Performance of music written by a dead composer was comparatively rare, and a whole concert consisting of such music would have been a significant anomaly.

Thus, in the musical practice of Medieval, Renaissance, and Baroque music, there was a significantly different way of *conceptualizing* music, in which the principal focus of music making was the *performance itself*. The idea of a musical work as an entity that was distinct and autonomous from the performance simply did not exist. Rather, pieces of music (to whatever extent they had an identity) were things that facilitated the activity of music making, not ends in themselves. As a result, performers and composers were united in a common task, which meant that there was no clear line of separation between composing and performing.

So what would music look like – or, rather, *sound* like – if our guiding ideal were that of making music together? In speaking of art and art works, William Desmond makes the helpful distinction between "encapsulating" and "participating."[42] In light of this distinction, we could say that the ideal of classical music has been primarily that of encapsulation: for composition is taken to be the setting into place of the boundaries of a work and thus performance will tend to be seen as essentially reproductive in the

---

[41] William Weber, "The Contemporaneity of Eighteenth-Century Musical Taste," *Musical Quarterly* 70 (1984) 175.

[42] William Desmond, *Art and the Absolute: A Study of Hegel's Aesthetics* (Albany: State University of New York Press, 1986) xix.

sense of following those boundaries. Yet, a participatory model presents us with a very different picture, in which performing and listening cannot be clearly separated from composition, precisely because they end up being part of the compositional process. Here I think the notion of improvisation helps in rethinking the binary opposition of composition and performance, for it gives us a notion of something that is *between* composition and performance.

But what *is* improvisation? Let's begin, again, by noting what it is *not*. Paul Berliner opens his monumental study of jazz improvisation with a quotation from the bassist Calvin Hill, who comments on his early conception of what constitutes jazz improvisation. "I used to think, How could jazz musicians pick notes out of thin air? I had no idea of the knowledge it took. It was like magic to me at the time."[43] To many people, improvisation *does* seem like magic. There are two important features to this (misguided) view of improvisation. First, the result of improvisation is taken to be a "work or structure produced on the spur of the moment."[44] In effect, it is a kind of "composing" done on the spot. Theoretically, we might be able to distinguish the "composition" of improvisation as the act of designating or selecting particular musical features and the "performance" of improvisation as the actual putting into sound of those features. However, practically, the distinction between the two is hardly clear. Since the composing and performing – the selecting and playing – occur simultaneously (or nearly so), it seems hard to say that the performance of these features in no way affects the selection of them (or vice versa). So, while the distinction is a useful and meaningful one (since it gets at two important and

[43] Paul Berliner, *Thinking in Jazz* (Chicago: University of Chicago Press, 1994) 1.
[44] *The Oxford English Dictionary*, 2nd ed., s.v. "improvisation."

not simply collapsible aspects of improvisation – that is, the aspect of "composing" and the aspect of "performing"), it is hard to take it as holding in a strong sense.

Second, the OED also gives us "the production or execution of anything offhand." Such a definition is certainly understandable etymologically, since "improvisation" has its roots in the Latin term "*improvisus*," which literally means "unforeseen." Of course, one might be tempted to respond here with the observation that dictionary makers aren't necessarily familiar with the improvisatory process. Yet, the *Harvard Dictionary of Music* (presumably compiled by lexicographers who are either musicians or else have some musical knowledge) tells us something similar, that improvisation is done "without the aid of manuscript, sketches or memory."[45] On both accounts, improvisation sounds almost like *creatio ex nihilo* – creation out of nothing. But is that really the case?

The problem with improvisation is that it does not fit very neatly into the schema that we normally use to think about music making – that is, the binary opposition of composition and performance.

On the one hand, improvisation seems at least to be a kind of extemporaneous composition in that it does not seem to be an "interpretation" of something that already exists. In this sense, it differs from performance, which we normally take to be a kind of *re-presentation* – the presentation of something that has already been present and is made present once again. That is hardly to say that we think of performance as being *wholly* repetitive; yet, we do take it as being *essentially* a kind of repetition in a way that improvisation is not. The result is that, while variations from performance to performance are not denied, they are still treated

---

[45] Willi Apel, *Harvard Dictionary of Music*, 2nd ed. (Cambridge, Mass.: Harvard University Press, 1969).

as more accidental than essential. A performance is essentially an *interpretation* of something that already exists, whereas improvisation presents us with something that only comes into being in the moment of its presentation.

On the other hand, improvisation fails to meet the requirements of a "true" composition. First, it does not seem to have the kind of premeditated or decided character that we think of musical works as having. Fully in line with this view, Stravinsky speaks of a musical work as being "the fruit of study, reasoning, and calculation that imply *exactly the converse of improvisation*."[46] Second, improvisations lack permanence, something that works are expected to have. True, recordings have significantly altered this situation, giving improvisation a kind of permanence they would not otherwise have. In fact, recordings clearly change the status of improvisations. For what was once a momentary phenomenon – never to be heard again, no matter how much one attempted to "duplicate" it – becomes a phenomenon that can be repeated over and over (even though the listeners may be different and the context may have dramatically changed). But the aural existence of an improvised solo does not have the same status as the written existence of a musical work, for the latter *prescribes* what ought to be the case whereas the former merely *describes* what once was the case in a particular performance.

It is precisely this characteristic of being *between* composition and performance that makes improvisation particularly well suited to thinking about both, as well as their relation to one another. On my view, both composition and performance are improvisatory in nature, albeit in different ways and to differing degrees. Composers never create *ex nihilo*, but instead "improvise": sometimes on tunes that already exist, but more frequently and importantly on the tradition in which they work.

---

[46] *Poetics of Music* 138 (my italics).

Performers – even when performing music that is strictly notated – do not merely "perform" but also "improvise" upon that which they perform.[47] Thus, there are many senses or levels of improvisation, probably so many as to make firm distinctions impossible. Yet, we can still divide improvisation into certain different types and degrees. Let me provide a few examples.

Improvisation$_1$: This sort of improvisation is the most "minimalistic." It consists of "filling-in" certain details that are not notated in the score. Such details include (but are not limited to) tempi, timbre, attack, dynamics, and (to some degree) instrumentation. No matter how detailed the score may be, some – and often much – improvisation of this sort is *necessary* simply in order to perform the piece. Thus *no* performance is possible without some form and degree of improvisation$_1$.

Improvisation$_2$: Although this level of improvisation is close to the previous one, it differs in that there is the addition of notes to the score that the performer is *expected* (by the composer) to supply. Two common forms of improvisation$_2$ are the addition of notes to complete a trill and the "filling-in" required by a score that only supplies figured bass.

Improvisation$_3$: The difference between improvisation$_3$ and improvisation$_2$ is purely quantitative. Rather than merely adding selected notes or filling out the chord, the performer adds measures or even whole sections. Examples include Baroque and Classical cadenzas, which the composer (again) expects the performer to supply. Sometimes these cadences are written out by the composer, with the expectation either that the performer follow them to the letter or else as a kind of guide or springboard for the performer's own improvising. In the case of the

---

[47] Godlovitch rightly claims (*Musical Performance* 83) that there is nothing about improvisation and performance that separates them "so utterly as to make them stand in radically different relations to the music made."

former, the performer then must decide whether to follow the supplied cadences or create something different (or improvise some admixture of the two).

Improvisation$_4$: In this case, a piece is transcribed for either a different instrument or different instruments, for voice (if originally for instruments), or for instruments (if originally for voice or voices). While the notes in the transcription may stay the same as in the original piece, often they are changed to accommodate the new instrument(s) or voice(s). However, usually the note relationships remain the same, meaning that the basic melody line and also the chords are unaltered. Transcriptions generally attempt to render the piece as close to the original as possible, making changes only when necessary (to accommodate different instruments or voices). However, not all transcriptions follow the original score in a strict sense. Depending on just how much a transcription varies from the original, it may become an instance of improvisation$_5$. Transcriptions, of course, can be done by the original composer or someone else.

Improvisation$_5$: This level of improvisation goes somewhat further than any of the previous ones, for the performer or conductor or an editor alters the score by adding or subtracting measures, passages, or even complete sections. Depending on the era of the composer, such alterations might be expected (as in Renaissance or Baroque music), allowed (as in some pieces by Beethoven), or explicitly (or implicitly) condemned (say, by a twentieth-century composer). Thus, such changes may or may not be expected by the composer. Those expected or approved could be designated improvisation$_{5a}$, with those not expected or approved designated as improvisation$_{5b}$.

Improvisation$_6$: It may – in at least certain cases – be difficult to make a clear-cut distinction between improvisation$_4$ and improvisation$_6$. Whereas the former attempts to render the score for other instruments or voices and may make some changes in the process, this sort is characterized by an explicit alteration known as "arranging." Arrangements can be minimal (and so very close to a transcription) or can be quite substantial – so much so that we might even begin to have questions as to whether we are still talking about the same piece of music. Note that transcriptions are often also arrangements (or vice versa), although arrangements are not necessarily transcriptions. One may, for instance, take a piece for piano and rearrange it for piano.

Improvisation$_7$: This sort of improvisation consists of altering the score (or, perhaps a "chart," a minimal score) by changing the melody line and/or altering the chords. Such improvisation is found in Baroque music and jazz. There are many variations of improvisation$_7$, such as:

improvisation$_{7a}$: the melody line is slightly changed, so that it is still clearly recognizable as, say, the Gershwin tune "A Foggy Day," but it does not strictly follow the sheet music version

improvisation$_{7b}$: a chord is altered enough to make it a different chord but still remain close enough to the original chord so that the new chord "fits" in the same place as the original chord. For instance, jazz musicians routinely alter the chord sequence in the third measure of "I Can't Get Started": instead of two beats each of E^7 and A minor, they play one beat each of B minor^7, E^7, B^bminor^7, and E^{b7}

improvisation$_{7c}$: the melody line is substantially changed, so that it is no longer completely clear to the listener whether there is any connection to the original melody

improvisation$_{7d}$: certain chords are changed substantially, although the basic chordal structure of the piece remains

improvisation$_{7e}$: the melody is completely disregarded and an alternative melody (or simply no discernible melody) is put in its place

Improvisation$_8$: Using the basic form of the score (such as a typical sixteen-bar blues piece), the performer improvises within those confines. In such a case, there may be no connection to the original melody, or even chords. Whereas the various forms of improvisation$_7$ had at least some connection to the original "piece," here there really is no discernible connection (at least to the listener, although possibly to the performer and the composer of the piece).

Improvisation$_9$: Whereas the first eight forms of improvisation are those of the performer, improvisation$_9$ is a compositional form of improvisation. Here the composer uses a particular form or style of music as a kind of template. Thus, Mozart's *Così fan tutte* depends on the *opera buffa* form, which has relatively strict requirements. How far requirements are followed, though, is subject to improvisation.

Improvisation$_{10}$: Here the composer takes a particular piece of music – a common folk tune (as in Aaron Copland's use of the Shaker melody "'Tis a Gift to Be Simple") or the composition of another composer (such as Handel's "borrowing" from other composers of his day) – and arranges it or uses it as the basis for a more complex or just simply different work. Whereas it is relatively easy to distinguish between Copland's reworking and the Shaker tune, sometimes the distinction between the material used and the reworked product is not so clear.

Improvisation$_{11}$: This is the most subtle form of improvisation. Both composer and performer are part of a musical tradition (perhaps classical, blues, or folk music) and they work within that tradition. But working within a tradition inevitably requires modifying that tradition by augmentation and transformation. One follows the rules of composition and performance; but composers and performers – particularly those we consider to be exemplary – also modify those rules and expectations. Therefore, the tradition is itself improvised upon. Any practice or discourse involves such improvisation.

By no means is this list meant to be exhaustive. These are only *some* of the forms and degrees that improvisation may take. I sketch these to show not only how varied improvisation can be but also how ever present it is in both "composition" and "performance." Thus, whereas a "performance" of a piece by Beethoven may not even appear to involve "improvisation" (since the improvisation is, comparatively speaking, minimal), the performance of a jazz tune (usually) necessitates an obvious sort of improvisation – as do many forms of non-Western music. But, even in such a case, more than one of these instances of improvisation is clearly involved.

At this point, I can certainly imagine that a reader might object to my use of the term "improvisation" to describe such a wide variety of musical activity. "Aren't there already terms (so such an objection might go) that describe these kinds of 'improvisation,' such as 'transcription' and 'arrangement'?" Certainly. Yet, the activities that I've described above turn out to be far less "widely varying" than one would be inclined to think – or so I will argue subsequently. In fact, what is interesting about the list given above is that the difference between the various forms of improvisation is far more *quantitative* than *qualitative*. Each instance involves a kind of reworking of something that *already* exists, so the differences concern the ways and the degrees to which this reworking takes place. Interestingly enough, *none* of these instances qualifies as "improvisation" in the sense we cited earlier ("something created on the spur of the moment out of nothing"). I will have much more to say about this aspect of spontaneous "creation" in both Chapter 2 and Chapter 4.

Of course, one might also object that my use of the term "improvisation" to describe the "performance" of the classical musician blurs the distinction between "performance" and "improvisation." Indeed it does; and that is precisely my intent. However, I think that such a blurring simply recognizes what is actually the case, despite the fact that we are inclined not to recognize the close proximity of improvisation, composition, and performance. Note that I am not suggesting that we jettison the use of the terms "composition" and "performance" and replace both with "improvisation" (nor am I suggesting that we abandon such terms or such notions as "transcription" or "arrangement"). Such terms are still useful (and, besides, they are relatively entrenched).[48] But I *do* mean to suggest that we should *think* of these entities (or, better yet, *activities*) in a different way, one that makes improvisation central to them. In this respect, I am sure to ruffle the feathers of any "ordinary language philosopher" who assumes that ordinary language provides the key for understanding the way things "really are." For, on my account, our musical terminology may not adequately reflect the reality of music making. Yet, if there is a conflict, it seems to me that the terminology – not the practice – should give way.

But there is another reason why I find the notion of improvisation particularly appropriate. On Martin Heidegger's account, creating a work of art is in effect the setting up of a world.[49] Although in "The Origin of the Work of Art," Heidegger primarily defines this idea of setting up a world in terms of truth, one can also read this idea in terms of his notion of "dwelling."[50] That is, the work of art provides a space in which to dwell. And

---

[48] Actually, they are not quite as firmly entrenched as we might think. "Transcription" and "arrangement" only go back to the nineteenth century (at least in their distinctly musical senses). See the *The Oxford English Dictionary*, 2nd ed., s.v. "arrangement" and "transcription."

[49] Wolterstorff argues for something similar in *Works and Worlds of Art*, though his conception of how these worlds exist and come into being differs from both Heidegger's account and my own.

[50] Martin Heidegger, "The Origin of the Work of Art," in *Poetry, Language, Thought*, trans. Albert Hofstadter (New York: Harper & Row, 1971).

that space is not merely for the artist but for others. Applying this musically, one way of thinking about a musical work is that it provides a world in which music making can take place. Performers, listeners, and even composers in effect dwell within the world it creates. And their way of dwelling is best characterized as "improvisation," in one or more senses of improvisation given above (and perhaps in senses *not* listed above).

How does this "dwelling" take place? Although we noted that the term "improvise" derives from the Latin "*improvisus*" (unforeseen) and so is at best only tangentially related to "improve" (which derives from the old French "*emprouer*," meaning "to invest profitably"), there is an interesting similarity. We can take an early meaning of "improvise" – "to fabricate out of what is conveniently on hand" – and connect it with an early meaning for "improve" – "to make profitable use of, to take advantage of, to inclose [*sic*] and cultivate (waste land); hence to make land more valuable or better by such means."[51] Dwelling, then, is not simply "taking up space." Rather, it necessarily transforms the space in which one dwells. Or we might say that, in dwelling, one must "fabricate out of what is conveniently on hand." Thus, both improvisation and improvement work with the given in order to "create" something new.

In the chapters that follow, I explore this improvisatory transformation that takes place in music making.

[51] *The Oxford English Dictionary*, 2nd ed., s.v. "improvise" and "improve" (respectively).

TWO

Composing

From Ursprung *to* Fassung letzter Hand

W HEN DOES A MUSICAL WORK FIRST APPEAR? IS IT BORN as a fully formed object or does it continue to develop after birth? If the latter, is there some identifiable point at which the composer (or perhaps someone else) declares its development "finished?" In this chapter, we will follow the movement from a musical work's origin (*Ursprung*) to its placement "in" a final text (what musicologists term the *Fassung letzter Hand* – the final manuscript).

For Husserl, ideal objects become truly ideal – which is to say, unchanging, permanent and available to all – by becoming embodied in written language. But, if writing serves merely to embody an ideal object, then that ideal object must have emerged and taken shape at some previous point. What stands as a prior step to an *Urtext*, then, is an *Ursprung* – a point of origin. Essential to Husserl's theory of ideal objects is the qualification that they are inherently historical: that is, they have an *Erstmaligkeit*, a point at which they first come into existence.[1]

---

[1] *Formal and Transcendental Logic* 81, and Jacques Derrida, *Edmund Husserl's* Origin of Geometry: *An Introduction*, trans. John P. Leavey (Stony Brook, N.Y.: Nicolas Hays, 1978) 48.

According to Husserl, the first glimmer of an inchoate ideal object emerges as an immediate experience – an idea or insight – in the mind of a particular person. What characterizes this insight is its clarity and "self-evidence."[2] Yet this instantaneous grasp can be extremely fleeting in nature and, in any case, has no permanent existence. Thus, the further steps – memory, speech, and written inscription – that constitute the ideal object crystallize this idea into an ideality, making it into something that can be passed on to others. It is important to note here that Husserl sees each of these steps as playing a role that is no more and no less than that of simply preserving the original idea unchanged.

We can think of this process of "creation" in terms of Husserl's conception of intentionality. There are, of course, at least two different senses in which the terms "intention" or "intentionality" can be used. The most common of these is the desire to act in a certain way or bring about a certain result. "I would like to compose an opera" is an example of this sort of intentionality, what we might call intentionality$_1$. Naturally, there might well be other intentions that accompany this (such as "I intend that, when my opera debuts at the Met, I will be assured of a place in the musical pantheon"). But Husserl's much broader use of the term describes the way in which the mind relates to an object. On his view, *all* mental acts are – by nature – intentional, since it's impossible to think without thinking *about* something. So when I think a thought or perceive an object, I "intend" that thought or object. We can term this intentionality$_2$. Of course, these two senses often go together. Thus, when I think of a particular object I may do so because I "intended" to think of that object (intentionality$_1$) and, in actually thinking about it, I "intend" it (intentionality$_2$).

[2] Edmund Husserl, "The Origin of Geometry," in *The Crisis of European Sciences and Transcendental Phenomenology: An Introduction to Phenomenological Philosophy*, trans. David Carr (Evanston, Ill.: Northwestern University Press, 1970) 359.

In the sense of intentionality$_2$, when we "intend" an object, that object is "present" to our minds. As should be clear, the level of presence to the mind can be greater or lesser. Husserl speaks of presence in terms of intentionality being "empty" or "filled," "vague" or "distinct."[3] The more filled and distinct a composer's intention is, the more "present" that object is to her mind. Or, to take a different example, I can know the name of a piece written by, say, Max Reger or John Lennon but have little or no idea what it sounds like. In such a case, that piece is only present to my mind in a "signitive" way (that is, I only know the name).

When E. D. Hirsch speaks of author's intentions, he is working from Husserl's account. Although Hirsch is speaking of literary texts when he argues for what he terms "the sensible belief that a text means what its author meant," that belief could easily be applied (*mutatis mutandis*) to musical texts.[4] Of course, this belief presupposes at least two things: (1) that an author or composer really knew what he intended and (2) was able to communicate that intention in such a way that others could understand it just as the author understood it.

But, if pieces of music can be described at least partially in terms of "intentions" on the part of a composer, how does the emergence of these intentions actually take place? Whereas for a philosopher or mathematician we would assume that it occurs in a moment of understanding, for a composer we tend to think of it in terms of *inspiration*. And there is good reason why we think in such terms. Not only has inspiration been a central romantic ideal but also two of our most revered composers appear to have spoken of their own composing in such terms.

---

[3] *Formal and Transcendental Logic* 56–62.
[4] E. D. Hirsch, Jr., *Validity in Interpretation* (New Haven, Conn.: Yale University Press, 1967) 1.

Ever since its publication in 1815, the letter of Mozart to the mysterious "Baron von..." has taken on an almost legendary significance and has been highly influential in forming our ideas not only about how Mozart's musical mind worked but how composers as a whole tend to create their works (even William James makes reference to this letter as an example of how great minds work).

> Concerning my way of composing... I can really say no more on this subject than the following; for I myself know no more about it, and cannot account for it. When I am, as it were, completely myself, entirely alone, and of good cheer – say, travelling in a carriage, or walking after a good meal, or during the night when I cannot sleep; it is on such occasions that my ideas flow best and most abundantly. *Whence* and *how* they come, I know not; nor can I force them.

Note how closely Beethoven's account parallels that of Mozart:

> You will ask me whence I take my ideas? That I cannot say with any degree of certainty: they come to me uninvited, directly or indirectly. I could almost grasp them in my hands, out in Nature's open, in the woods, during my promenades, in the silence of the night, at the earliest dawn.[5]

Of course, as Maynard Solomon makes clear, both of these accounts are fabrications. But they fit perfectly with the image of the creative genius. The letter supposed to have been written by Mozart was actually penned and published by Friedrich Rochlitz, one of Mozart's admirers. Rather than describing Mozart's actual compositional process, Rochlitz (who happened to have been greatly influenced by Kant) was instead describing

---

5 Maynard Solomon, "Beethoven's Creative Process: A Two-Part Invention," in Maynard Solomon, *Beethoven Essays* (Cambridge, Mass.: Harvard University Press, 1988) 128–9.

the romantic *ideal* of the creative process. Given Mozart's then sagging popularity, nothing could have been more effective than the shrewd media image of the artistic genius whose masterpieces simply floated effortlessly into his head. Furthermore, the reason for the similarity of Beethoven's account to that of Mozart is no more complicated than that Louis Schlösser paraphrased Rochlitz's letter, adding a few details along the way to give it the ring of authenticity.

It is a little disappointing that these accounts turn out to be spurious. We noted in the previous chapter that Levinson claims "there is a special aura that envelops composers, as well as other artists, because we think of them as true creators."[6] We do indeed tend to see composers as involved (to quote Levinson) in a kind of "godlike activity" and it is this we take to be characteristic of true artistic genius. Although Kant was certainly not the first to speak of genius, not only does the artistic genius play a central role in defining fine art for Kant but also Kant has in turn played a central role in defining what counts as fine art for us. What marks genius for Kant is the ability to see beyond the limits of the old ideas and allow the imagination free reign. Given that "a genius is nature's favorite," it is through genius that the rule of art is shaped.[7] Of course, the genius is not in the business of following the rules but of breaking them – and so creating new ones. On Kant's account, what genius creates is: (1) original, in the sense of never having existed before; (2) exemplary, as something that provides a rule for others to follow; and (3) beyond scientific description. But how exactly does the genius go about creating these new rules? Precisely that is the rub. For, if Kant is

---

[6] "What a Musical Work Is" 67.

[7] Immanuel Kant, *Critique of Judgment*, trans. Werner S. Pluhar (Indianapolis: Hackett, 1987) 187 [§49].

right, then even the genius is as much in the dark as the rest of us.

> Genius itself cannot describe or indicate scientifically how it brings about its products, and it is rather as *nature* that it gives the rule. That is why, if an author owes a product to his genius, he himself does not know how he came by the ideas for it; nor is it in his power to devise such products at his pleasure, or by following a plan, and to communicate [his procedure] to others in precepts that would enable them to bring about like products.[8]

Clearly there *is* something slightly mysterious about creating a piece of music or a piece of sculpture; and the attempt to describe this process in detail is probably hopeless from the start. As pseudo-Mozart and pseudo-Beethoven tell us, neither of them really know where their musical ideas come from: they simply appear. This seems to be a relatively universal phenomenon: Copland speaks of a musical theme as being "a gift from heaven," for the composer "doesn't know where it comes from – has no control over it."[9] Moreover, anyone who has created virtually anything (musical, literary, mechanical, or otherwise) has had this experience. One gets ideas. Creation is something that, in at least one sense and a truly important one at that, just happens. To the extent that a creation goes beyond the rules and so is an "original," it has nothing to fall back on for explanation. It can only point to the new rules that it has indirectly created. Or so goes Kant's essentially romantic explanation.

On the other hand, this account of creation is, for Kant, in strong contrast to his account of discovery. Whereas Kant sees *creation* as inherently unfathomable, he considers the act of *discovery* – that is, what a scientist does – as fully explicable.[10]

---

[8] Ibid. 175 [§46].
[9] *What to Listen for in Music* 23.
[10] *Critique of Judgment* 176–7 [§47].

Unlike a poet or composer, Newton was able to explain his discoveries well enough that others could understand how he arrived at them. Yet, are discovery and creation really so very different from one another? Moreover, to what extent is it possible to say (as does Levinson) that "the artist brings into being what did not exist beforehand?"[11]

In contrast to Levinson, Kivy argues that composers are actually engaged in *discovery* rather than *creation*. On his view, musical works have somehow always existed. Whether Kivy's musical Platonism can be justified is itself an interesting question, but my concern here is his attack on Levinson's assumption of the "originality" of musical composition. As Kivy notes, the kind of discoveries that Newton made were hardly less creative than the works that Mozart created. And he (rightly) argues that in Kant we end up with "a hideous caricature of scientific discovery."[12]

So what, then, is it to *create* something? Is it really the same as *discovery*? Part of the difficulty here is that we sometimes speak of composers as making discoveries in the sense of discovering, say, how to make a particular passage work musically. But it is more complicated than this: for creation always involves some sense of discovery and discovery is likewise unthinkable apart from creation. Kivy observes that "Gödel discovered the theorem which bears his name. But he had to invent Gödel numbering to do it."[13] Thus, there seems to be some sort of connection between the two aspects. Yet, is there not something important lacking in Kivy's account? True, Gödel may have discovered his theorem, but he did not just discover it in the sense that one discovers a rock. What is crucial here is that discoveries always take place

---

[11] "What a Work of Art Is" 66.
[12] Peter Kivy, "Platonism in Music: A Kind of Defense," in Peter Kivy, *The Fine Art of Repetition: Essays in the Philosophy of Music* (Cambridge: Cambridge University Press, 1993) 38 and 42.
[13] Ibid. 39.

within a very definite context. Indeed, it is precisely that context that not only makes a discovery or creation possible but also causes us to construe it *as* a discovery or creation. In other words, what *counts* as a discovery is contextually determined. John Fisher points out that when we say that Watson and Crick discovered the double helix what we mean is "that they discovered that the structure of DNA is a double helix."[14] But do we not actually mean *more* than that? Don't we mean not only that Watson and Crick "saw" this structure but that they also saw the *significance* of it? Discovery is not just seeing. It is seeing something *as* significant. Anyone else might have observed this structure, but it was Watson and Crick who realized not only what they were seeing but that it was important – or at least it was deemed important *by them*. Thus, in a wider sense, it was deemed significant *from within the context of a given community*, in this case the community of twentieth-century scientists. It seems quite possible to imagine another community having seen the same thing and not finding it significant, for whatever reason. In such a case it would simply not count as a discovery. Indeed, we might even go so far as to say that "it" might end up being "nothing at all." On the other hand, we take "it" to be a discovery precisely because we *do* find it significant, and that is closely connected to the fact that we think it is *useful* for our ends. Furthermore, note that in discovering his theorem, Gödel did not just discover something that was merely "out there"; instead that theorem is a way of *thinking about* reality that owes as much to Gödel's own creative thought as it does to the phenomenon that he discovered. Gödel's discovery, then, is equally a kind of creation.

How exactly does this relate to musical composition, though? What seems to be neglected in Levinson's conception of the

---

[14] John Fisher, "Discovery, Creation, and Musical Works," *Journal of Aesthetics and Art Criticism* 49 (1991) 133.

composer is that music is always something that takes place *within* a community and thus is inherently what we might term "practice-," "discourse-," or "tradition-" related.[15] On Alasdair MacIntyre's account, a practice is a social activity regulated by goals and standards.[16] Clearly, music making is such a practice, although there are different practices within the wider practice of music making. Practices are, in turn, situated within wider traditions that make sense of those practices and relate them to other practices.[17]

Of course, practices are also regulated in various ways. Foucault reminds us that – in any practice – "we are not free to say just anything...when we like or where we like."[18] Both composers and performers working in a particular musical practice have relatively defined boundaries as to what is or is not allowed – in terms of harmony, style, length, and many other factors. A classical composer writing today could, for instance, write something that had a distinct rhythm and blues feel. But that "feel" would have to be set in an idiom that at least resembled something

---

[15] Alastair MacIntyre's idea of a "practice" and Michel Foucault's notion of a "discourse" are clearly *not* synonymous, although they are both useful (since each emphasizes certain important aspects). One significant difference between them, of course, is that Foucault is particularly concerned with the ways in which social activities are regulated and power exercised. See, for instance, his essay "The Discourse on Language" in Michel Foucault, in *The Archaeology of Knowledge*, trans. A. M. Sheridan Smith (New York: Pantheon, 1972) 215–37. My comments on discourses are drawn primarily from this essay.

[16] Alastair MacIntyre, *After Virtue*, 2nd ed. (Notre Dame, Ind.: University of Notre Dame Press, 1981) 190.

[17] See Wolterstorff's "The Work of Making a Work of Music," in Philip Alperson, *What is Music?: An Introduction to the Philosophy of Music* (University Park: Pennsylvania State University Press, 1994). I take this essay to represent a significant change in his position, at least in the sense that it depicts the making of musical works as taking place within a musical practice.

[18] "The Discourse on Language" 216.

like classical music. On the other hand, the practice *itself* could change (though probably not from this one instance), since practices are historical and so in flux. What is "appropriate" for a classical composer *today* is remarkably different today from what it was two centuries ago. Think of what Haydn could have written and what, say, Charles Koechlin was able to write. Even the difference between Debussy and Stockhausen (two twentieth-century composers) is remarkable.

In addition, discourses (or practices) have certain texts – and, thus, composers – that are taken to be authoritative. One cannot compose something that wanders *too* far from those texts and their basic styles and expectations. Yet, discourses always have some "space" between the authoritative texts and the sorts of "commentaries" that are allowed. Commentaries can be defined as new texts that are created (so Puccini's *Madame Butterfly* can be heard as a "commentary" on his earlier *La Bohème*, on Verdi, on the genre of Italian opera and opera in general). But we can just as easily think of performances as commentaries on the works that are performed. Whether wide or narrow, that "space" between texts and other texts or between texts and performances is what allows a discourse to expand and change.

A composer, then, does not compose in a social vacuum but within a rather firmly defined social practice. In fact, we could take this even further and say that – outside of such a practice – this activity would likely make little sense: that is, it would not be seen as *significant* activity, or else it might have a very different significance. Thus, composing never occurs in the way that (as Levinson would have it) "a demiurge forms a world out of inchoate matter" and so cannot be seen as resulting in anything that is even remotely close to "absolute newness."[19] Even the

---

[19] "What A Musical Work Is" 66–7.

avant-garde Pierre Boulez acknowledges that composing always takes place within a tradition:

> The composer is exactly like you, constantly on the horns of the same dilemma, caught in the same dialectic – the great models and an unknown future. He cannot take off into the unknown. When people tell me, "I am taking off into the unknown and ignoring the past" it is complete nonsense.[20]

Of course, Levinson himself emphasizes the fact that compositions arise in a historical context (for he explicitly wishes to argue against the thesis that musical works have an eternal existence); it is just that he does not seem to appreciate the full implications of the historicality of musical works.

Rather than working with "inchoate matter," then, musical composition is limited by constraints. Composers may be able to conceive new rhythms and chord progressions, but these are usually improvisations upon current rhythms and chord progressions. The Beatles, for instance, give us a wonderful example of how such far-ranging influences as Celtic music, rhythm and blues, and country and western could be put together in a new way.[21] So composers are dependent on the "languages" available to them and usually those languages are relatively well defined. What we call "innovation" comes either from pushing the boundaries of a language or from mixing elements of one language with another. Even such factors as what sorts of instruments happen to exist (or can be created) and the capabilities of performers are constraints with which composers must work.[22]

---

[20] Pierre Boulez, *Orientations: Collected Writings*, trans. Martin Cooper, ed. Jean-Jacques Nattiez (Cambridge, Mass.: Harvard University Press, 1986) 454.

[21] See Terence J. O'Grady, *The Beatles: A Musical Evolution* (Boston: Twayne, 1983).

[22] Of course, composers can sometimes come up with remarkable ways for using existing objects as "instruments." Malcolm Arnold's "A Grand

Precisely because composers and authors work within a musical discourse that is historically and culturally framed, it is difficult to know exactly how to classify their activity. Fisher asks: "Did Shakespeare discover or create the line 'To be or not to be: that is the question'? . . . In the sense in which no one can create a sentence, no one can create a sound structure. But it seems no more sensible to say that speakers *discover* sentences either."[23] So what exactly was involved in writing that memorable line? While Shakespeare likely created that line, it counts as creation only in a certain sense. Shakespeare did not create the English language, nor the meaning of those specific words. Indeed, there is every reason to suppose that something akin or even identical to this line had been created by some other speaker of English before – or it may even have been a common saying that Shakespeare merely filched. In any case, it was Shakespeare (or, given the way in which the texts that we label "Shakespearean" actually came into existence, just as likely an actor in his company or even an editor) who came up with the line as we know it.[24] Or perhaps what we should rather say is that "Shakespeare" took that line (whatever its origin) and imbued it with a certain significance by placing it within a particular context. In that sense, then, Shakespeare "discovered" a possible way of shaping the English language. But he clearly also created something – by "composing" the line out of preexisting words and by placing it within a particular context. Just as important,

Overture" uses three Hoover vacuums ("tuned" to different pitches) and an electric floor polisher (on "Hoffnung's Music Festivals," EMI CMS 7 63302-2).

[23] "Discovery, Creation, and Musical Works" 131.

[24] We must not forget that the idea of *specifying* the exact author (that is, to whom a text "belongs") is, in regard to literature (and *also* to music), a relatively modern idea. See Michel Foucault, "What is an Author?" in Michel Foucault, *Aesthetics, Method, and Epistemology* (*Essential Works of Foucault*, Vol. II), ed. James D. Faubion (1998) 205–22.

in so doing, he likewise helped shape the English language itself.

The problem here is that neither creation nor discovery seems quite adequate to describe the process of composing either literary or musical works. But *improvisation* very nicely captures both of these aspects. To improvise is to rework something that already exists (that is, "conveniently on hand") and thus transform it into something that both has connections to what it once was but now has a new identity. "Composing" is not simply a matter of bringing elements together; rather, they are brought together in a way that transforms those elements. To be sure, defining composition as improvisational "putting together" cannot help but bring the composer down to size. However, as Kivy points out, it is precisely the "wish to puff up the composer and his works that has led to most of the extravagant theories of music in the past, and the present as well."[25]

How is it possible, though, to reconcile this concept of composition as improvisational with the undeniable fact that composers get flashes of inspiration? One question here concerns where those inspirational flashes come from. Copland would have us believe that they come from heaven – and perhaps they sometimes do. But, if so, they seem to take a slight detour along the way.[26] In fact, many composers' ideas come from a much less mysterious source: they get them from each other. Charles Rosen notes that composers can influence one another in many different ways, with plagiarism on one extreme and an inspiration that is so subtle that it betrays no apparent points of similarity on the

---

[25] "Platonism in Music: A Kind of Defense," in *The Fine Art of Repetition* 45.

[26] One composer writes: "At one time I expected inspiration to come down like a bolt from the blue, but found that when it came it was only a brief fragment which dug its heels in and resisted any attempt to make it go forward." See Reginald Smith Brindle, *Musical Composition* (Oxford: Oxford University Press, 1986) 4.

other.[27] It is this last sort of influence that is perhaps the most profound.

But the most obvious sense in which composers have been dependent upon their predecessors or contemporaries is that of creative "borrowing," which we today would tend to call plagiarism.[28] Handel was unquestionably the most famous of these borrowers, taking passages and even whole pieces from composers such as Josquin, Muffat, and a great assortment of others (most of whom would not be very familiar to us today). For instance, out of the sixty-three segments of *Israel in Egypt*, sixteen betray a heavy debt to pieces by other composers.[29] So are those segments "new" pieces? Here our intuitions are left somewhat baffled. And Handel is simply the most obvious case: Bach took the theme for the *C Minor Fugue* from Johann Mattheson; Rossini borrowed an aria in *The Barber of Seville* from Haydn; and many composers have taken musical ideas from fellow composers or else simply transformed popular songs of their time. What we think of today as deeply moving "sacred" music, "O Welt, ich muß dich lassen" (from Bach's *St. Matthew Passion*) and "Jesu, meine Freude," began life as the considerably more mundane "Innsbruck, ich muß dich lassen" and "Flora, meine Freude," which celebrated a somewhat different sort of joy.

The connection of composers to the tradition, however, usually takes a far less obvious form. For instance, Rosen demonstrates

[27] Charles Rosen, "Influence: Plagiarism and Inspiration," in *On Criticizing Music: Five Philosophical Perspectives*, ed. Kingsley Price (Baltimore: Johns Hopkins University Press, 1981) 17.

[28] The fact that we today would refer to this as "idea theft" again reflects our belief that composers "own" their compositions, an idea that represents a profound change from the practice of borrowing once the norm.

[29] Handel also borrowed extensively from his own compositions. Speaking of the *Concerti a due cori*, Stanley Sadie observes that "all the music of the first two concertos is in fact adapted from earlier material." See the notes to The English Concert's recording of Handel's orchestral works (Archiv 423 149-2).

in detail how much Brahms was indebted to other composers, such as Chopin and Beethoven. A further example might be that of Mozart and the *opera buffa* tradition, which was governed by a set of conventions concerning aspects as diverse as length, character types, plots, and musical parameters. John Platoff notes that "Mozart could no more stand outside of these conventions than a brilliant Hollywood director of today...can ignore the commercial realities of modern filmmaking." Thus, when we examine Mozart's compositional process in light of what other composers of the time were doing, we find that what might seem to be a mysterious stroke of genius is far from enigmatic. Operas such as *Le nozze di Figaro* and *Così fan tutte* turn out to be perfect examples of *opera buffa*. In fact, what is surprising is how closely he follows the standard conventions of the form (going so far as to imitate an aria from a similar opera of the period). Yet, even in following those conventions he is likewise "altering, subverting or transcending them" – which is to say, improvising on them.[30] As long as we are generally unfamiliar with the musical practice in which Mozart was working, we find it difficult to see the path that he took; but, upon examining that framework, many compositional decisions become understandable.

What is most significant, though, is the improvisation that takes place along the way. Whereas Copland uses the exquisite Shaker melody " 'Tis a Gift to Be Simple" in his ballet *Appalachian Spring,* he molds it into something that is clearly distinctive and that bears his own stamp. Similarly, Handel, Bach, and Mozart all take the same opening notes (perhaps best remembered as the first four notes of the chorus "And with His Stripes" from Handel's *Messiah*) and make something remarkably different out of them (Bach in No. 20 of the *Forty-Eight Preludes and Fugues* [Book Two]

---

[30] John Platoff, "How Original Was Mozart?: Evidence from *opera buffa,*" *Early Music* 20 (1992) 105–6.

and Mozart in the "Kyrie" from his *Requiem*). Thus, even when composers use the material of others, what takes place is a *transformation* of that material – the elusive mixture of *imitatio* and *variatio* that constitutes improvisation. Or, to take an example from another genre, Charlie Parker improvised "Scrapple from the Apple" out of "Honeysuckle Rose."

Precisely this aspect of "improvising" is something that our theories of artistic creation tend to downplay – or simply ignore. And there is good reason for this: it simply does not fit well with the notion of composer as creator. The suggestion that composing is inherently improvisational makes composers seem far less like isolated individuals and their compositions not nearly so autonomous. Composing, then, is not taking oneself out of the community but, rather, taking part in it. It is significant that Stravinsky speaks of getting the composing process going by "sometimes playing old masters (to put myself in motion)."[31] That is not to say that composers do not have flashes of inspiration. Yet, not only does that inspiration arise within a specific musical framework, but even what would count as genuine inspiration (for inspiration is clearly a *normative* concept – that is, what we accept as inspiration is only something that we assume to be valuable) is inevitably going to be determined by the collective taste of the community. What a composer "discovers" are ways of putting notes, chords, and themes together that sound pleasing to her and the result is judged to be "inspired" or not depending on how it pleases the community of composers, performers, and listeners. Admittedly, the initial response may be tepid or even cool, but if no one – either then or at a later point – recognizes that piece as "inspired" then it would be hard to continue to maintain that it is.

[31] Igor Stravinsky and Robert Craft, *Conversations with Igor Stravinsky* (Berkeley and Los Angeles: University of California Press, 1980) 16.

Furthermore, if we say that Wagner "discovered" the Tristan chord what we clearly do not mean is that he *simply* came across a relation of notes that had always existed (of course, as it turns out the Tristan chord had already been, in at least some sense, "discovered" by someone else).[32] Fisher is right in saying that "only Wagner could have 'discovered' his Tristan chord because only Wagner had that style and that set of interests. Only Wagner could choose to give that chord and its related motives their particular use and meaning."[33] But the reason that we can say this is because Wagner did not so much discover this chord as give it a special significance that it never had before, in the same way that Shakespeare imbued the line "To be or not to be" with a significance it likely never had. Of course, it must likewise be emphasized that Wagner's "style" and "set of interests" are themselves deeply embedded in and indebted to the musical tradition of the nineteenth century and only make sense within that context. They are Wagner's, but only in a limited sense. Moreover, *we* are able to hear the Tristan chord *as* a beautiful harmonic structure, but that is only because *our* hearing patterns have been established in a particular direction. People from other times and cultures might just as easily hear it as insufferable noise (and, of course, some of Wagner's contemporaries did on occasion categorize his music as just that).

Not only do the contours of a given musical discourse provide the materials for composition, they also play a tremendous role in determining how composers go about composing. For instance,

[32] Musicologists long ago noted the similarity between a chord in Spohr's *Der Alchymist* (1830) and the "Wagner" chord. But Wagner makes the chord his own. As Roland Jackson puts it, "Spohr's Italian sixth chord is turned [by Wagner] into a more intense French sixth," and then given a slightly different resolution. See Roland Jackson, "*Leitmotive* and Form in the *Tristan* Prelude," in *Prelude and Transfiguration from Tristan and Isolde*, ed. Robert Bailey (New York: W.W. Norton, 1985) 268–9.

[33] "Discovery, Creation, and Musical Works" 135.

although Mozart was a remarkably quick composer, this can to some extent be explained.[34] Leonard Meyer observes that

> Mozart could compose with astonishing facility partly because the set of constraints he inherited (and that he partly modified), the so-called Classical style, was especially coherent, stable, and well-established. As a result, Mozart had to make relatively few deliberate choices among alternatives.[35]

As long as the limitations of a musical discourse are clear, the composer is forced (or, we might rather say, is *free*) to make far fewer choices. Constraints can be wonderfully freeing. Meyer likewise notes that the compositional processes of both Bartók and Schoenberg were considerably more difficult precisely "because the styles they employed required them to make many more conscious, time-consuming decisions."[36] Or, to put that another way: both of them were working within a musical discourse that was far less defined and coherent than that of Mozart; and, while that allowed them far more freedom in one sense, it made their task all the more difficult.

As surprising as it might seem, the recognition that musical works only arise from *within* a musical community does in one way point us back to Kant. For, although Kant begins by telling us that genius creates rather than follows the rules and is characterized by allowing the imagination free reign, his account of genius is complicated by the element of taste. True, genius is required for *producing* art, whereas taste is what guides aesthetic judgment; but even genius cannot produce art simply on the basis

---

[34] That should perhaps also be qualified in another sense: for however easy composing may have been for Mozart (at least in comparison to other composers), note that he described the Haydn Quartets as "il frutto di una lunga, e laboriosa fatica" [the fruit of a prolonged and difficult labor].

[35] Leonard B. Meyer, *Style and Music: Theory, History, and Ideology* (Philadelphia: University of Pennsylvania Press, 1989) 5.

[36] Ibid.

of unbridled imagination, for fine art needs taste as a kind of corrective.

> The artist, having practiced and corrected his taste by a variety of examples from art or nature, holds his work up to it, and, after many and often laborious attempts to satisfy his taste, finds that form which is adequate to it. Hence this form is not, as it were, a matter of inspiration or of a free momentum of the mental powers; the artist is, instead, slowly and rather painstakingly touching the form up in an attempt to make it adequate to his thought while yet keeping it from interfering with the freedom in the play of these powers.[37]

What Kant admits, then, is that genius is not simply out on its own. Production would seem to be impossible without taste. He later goes on to say that "insofar as art shows genius it does indeed deserve to be called *inspired* [*geistreich*], but it deserves to be called *fine* art only insofar as it shows taste." How taste serves to keep genius in check is that "it severely clips its wings, and makes it civilized, or polished."[38]

Perhaps the most surprising turnabout, though, is Kant's conclusion that "if there is a conflict between these two properties in a product, and something has to be sacrificed, then it should rather be on the side of genius."[39] If taste has the final say over genius, though, genius must be bound by at least some rules: for taste must inevitably be itself defined in terms of at least some rules, however general, indefinite, or changing they may be. That is not to say that genius does not break rules, for "some deviation of the common rule" is appropriate; but this seems a far milder statement than some of Kant's earlier ones.[40] Indeed, in these passages on taste, Kant depicts the artist much more as *improviser*

---

[37] *Critique of Judgment* 180–1 [§48].
[38] Ibid. 188 (§50).
[39] Ibid.
[40] Ibid. 187 (§49).

on the rules than as *ex nihilo* creator of them. The artist, then, is one who both works within rules and, at the same time, effectively modifies them. Given the importance of taste, perhaps we could say that true genius lies in not being too much of one. To become a composer is not merely to have flashes of inspiration but to learn how to channel that inspiration. Even Kant recognizes that "genius can only provide rich *material* for products of fine art; processing this material and giving it *form* requires a talent that is academically trained."[41] Thus, even the genius's so-called inspiration is no less a result of the influences of the musical practice in which it arises.

Of course, if the composer is at once following and improvising upon those rules, new compositions are inevitably going to influence taste. Composers do not merely work *within* a given discourse: the act of composition inevitably involves going beyond the lines. Composition is both the improvisation of music and the improvisation on that discourse. Not only do composers provide new ways of applying the conventions of a given discourse but also they may reshape those conventions.

By replacing the "creation model" of composing with an *improvisational model*, I think we have both a more phenomenologically accurate picture of what actually takes place in making music and a more balanced view of the relation between artist and community – one in which it is actually possible to see the artist as an integral part of the community.

Die Fassung letzter Hand

Few of us can forget Milos Forman's depiction of the composer Salieri in the film *Amadeus*. What filled Salieri with jealousy was the effortless way in which Mozart went about composing, as

[41] Ibid. 178 [§47].

was particularly evidenced in his supposedly perfect and unre-
touched scores. Once again, the basis for this idea is at least partly
that apocryphal letter, in which "Mozart" (that is, Rochlitz) writes:

> Provided I am not disturbed, my subject enlarges itself, and I
> expand it ever wider and ever clearer; and the whole, though
> it be long, stands almost complete and finished in my head, so
> that I can survey it in my mind, like a fine picture or a comely
> form at a glance.... When I proceed to write down my ideas, I
> take out of the bag of my memory, if I may use that phrase, what
> has previously been collected into it in the way that I have men-
> tioned. For this reason the committing to paper is done quickly
> enough, for everything is, as I said before, already finished; and
> it rarely differs on paper from what it was in my imagination.

Schlösser likewise imitated this description, making "Beethoven"
say:

> I carry my thoughts about with me for a long time, sometimes
> a very long time, before I set them down. At the same time
> my memory is so faithful to me that I am sure not to forget
> a theme which I have once conceived, even after years have
> passed. I make many changes, reject and reattempt until I am
> satisfied. Then the working-out in breadth, length, height and
> depth begins in my head, and since I am conscious of what
> I want, the basic idea never leaves me. It rises, grows upward,
> and I hear and see the picture as a whole take shape and stand
> forth before me in my mind as though cast in a single piece,
> so that all that is left is the work of writing it down. This goes
> quickly.[42]

If these are highly romanticized pictures of composing, then
what exactly *is* involved in the improvisational "putting together"

---

[42] "Beethoven's Creative Process" 127–8. Note that Beethoven himself had
(quite disingenuously) claimed in a letter: "I merely jot down certain
ideas...and when I have completed the whole in my head, everything is
written down, but only once." See *The Letters of Beethoven*, Vol. II, trans.
Emily Anderson (London, 1961) no. 1060.

known as composing? We tend to assume that there is a specific sort of artistic process common to all artists and composers. Artur Schnabel claimed, for example, that "the process of artistic creation is always the same – from *inwardness* to *lucidity*."[43] Clearly, though, there must be significant differences in how composers get to this point of lucidity, as well as just how lucid it actually is. An important part of this difference is how freely and spontaneously composers work. On one side of the spectrum is a composer like Schubert, who supposedly churned out a song per day. Gershwin significantly surpassed this record, since "he wrote six songs a day to get the bad ones out of his system."[44] Perhaps he did. However, some of these accounts seem more designed to fit with the romantic ideal: for the reality in most cases is that inspiration is far outweighed by struggle and hard work. One begins to understand just how difficult that labor may be when one realizes, for instance, that Elliott Carter filled two thousand pages worth of manuscripts for what ended up as the sixty-two-page text of his String Quartet No. 2. Wolterstorff is right in claiming that we are greatly in need of "a new model of the process of artistic composition in which both the working and the waiting find a place."[45]

How, then, might we characterize the process of creation? In Chapter 1, we noted that Wolterstorff wishes to draw a line between improvisation and composition. An organist improvising at the organ is not composing a work precisely because "in all likelihood he did not, during his improvising, finish selecting that particular set of requirements for correctness of occurrence to be found in the score." But is not the organist *in the process of composing* while at the organ? Despite the fact that the

---

[43] Roger Sessions, *The Musical Experience of Composer, Performer, Listener* (Princeton, N.J.: Princeton University Press, 1950) 45.

[44] See Michael Feinstein's notes to Dave Grusin's "The Gershwin Connection" (GRP-2005 2).

[45] "The Work of Making a Work of Music" 105.

organist writes this down later, the process of composition would seem to have begun at the point of improvisation. Although it is well known that many composers – from Buxtehude and Bach through Mozart and Beethoven to Hummel and Liszt – were also famed improvisers, that fact has been generally seen as having little impact on their work as "composers." But is it really possible to separate Bach the improviser from Bach the composer? Indeed, there is every reason to think that many of his compositions began as improvisations at the keyboard – and were in turn improvised on.

So it would seem that, at least in many cases, the selection process is one that takes place over time, and may even involve a number of phases. In other words, the compositional process itself tends to be a kind of improvisational process: one begins with certain ideas or themes and improvises on them until something results. Earlier we noted that Stravinsky often sought inspiration by listening to his predecessors, but it also is instructive that he goes on to say that he also works by "sometimes starting directly to improvise rhythmic units on a provisional row of notes." Yet, if compositions often *start* with some motif (whether a particular theme, a chord progression, or even something like Wagner's Tristan chord), how do they develop from there? Susanne Langer characterizes the first stage of composition as "a more or less sudden recognition of the total form to be achieved" and "this form is the 'composition' that [the composer] feels called upon to develop."[46] What Langer seems to imply here is that the idea for a composition appears in "kernel" form: that is, the idea that the composer has is like a seed that already contains within it the pattern for its development. Yet, is this how compositions develop? Perhaps in some cases it is. One could argue that within

[46] Susanne K. Langer, *Feeling and Form* (New York: Charles Scribner's Sons, 1953) 121.

the Tristan chord is a kind of pattern that in some sense dictated the development of *Tristan und Isolde*. But the level of that "dictation" would seem to be rather minimal.

Of course, for most of us it is difficult to know what to make of Langer's account or any other for that matter, since artistic creation seems relatively mysterious. Simply put: few of us have actually written any music ourselves. Still, almost all of us have at least some idea of what *writing* involves: the frustration of deciding how to begin, the overflowing wastebasket (now replaced by the overflowing delete file), the working and reworking of passages (and *still* not being satisfied with them), the lack of knowing at the beginning exactly how all of this is going to turn out in the end, and the final version that is declared "final" simply because of a deadline. While one usually (although not always) has a central thesis or point in mind in writing something, the written text often takes on a kind of life of its own, sometimes evolving with each version into something that one never envisioned.[47] Thus, despite Husserl's conception of the stage of writing as providing no more than a written embodiment for what had already been created, it seems likely that the process of writing would itself play an important part in shaping the contours of a musical work. Only rarely do we write something in which the actual writing process does not in some way serve to formulate, reformulate, or sharpen our ideas. Indeed, it is not an infrequent experience to find that one's views have changed remarkably in the writing process, sometimes so much that we no longer agree with our original thesis.

Arguing against Wolterstorff's view that an organist in the process of improvising is not also in the process of composing, Kivy

[47] It is not uncommon for writers to speak of being amazed by what the protagonists of their novels end up doing and saying, as well as how their characters develop.

provides the example of Bach, who improvised a *ricercare* (which was to become part of *Musikalisches Opfer*) while visiting Frederick the Great. On arriving home, Bach put this down on paper from memory – or so tradition has it. What Kivy wants to argue is that it seems plausible to think that Bach was actually composing this *ricercare* while he was improvising it. On that point, Kivy seems right. However, what seems rather implausible is Kivy's suggestion that, in writing it down, "Bach was merely (!) being his own copyist, recording in notation from his memory of what he had played: a prodigious feat, needless to say."[48] Truly that would be a prodigious feat – and perhaps slightly beyond belief. But, assuming that Bach *could* have written down exactly what he had played (not one note more and not one note less, without any variation *whatever*), is there any reason to think that he *would* have? In short, are we to assume that Bach would have been so satisfied (perhaps we should say so "self-satisfied") with what he had played that he would not have wanted to change *anything*? That does indeed stretch the imagination. Since this story is based on tradition, of course, we have no way of knowing one way or the other; and traditional accounts tend to stress the miraculous. Yet, I think it is far more plausible to imagine that Bach did not *merely* copy out the *ricercare* but was actively involved in reshaping it as he did, perhaps quite significantly. In fact, Bach may have written it out multiple times and tried many different versions (perhaps also in performance): we simply do not know. But, if other composers are any guide, something along that line would seem far more likely. To use another traditional story, it is interesting that Mozart is said to have tried out various versions of the Overture to *Don Giovanni* on his friends in order to see which they liked better. What that would seem to suggest is that Mozart himself

---

[48] "Platonism in Music: A Kind of Defense," *The Fine Art of Repetition* 53 (the exclamation point is Kivy's).

was not quite sure and thought the opinion of others might be helpful in deciding.

That composing musical scores is very much a *process* becomes evident when we consider the issue of the composer's intentions. It seems safe to assume that composers have intentions concerning their compositions – or else they would never have bothered to write them in the first place. We may not always know what they are, but we can usually make relatively informed conjectures. Yet, what sorts of intentions do composers have and just how defined are they? Clearly, the intentions of composers are both varied and formed in light of the musical practice in which they work. In composing a particular piece, composers may have such diverse intentions as conquering a musical challenge, trying a new style of music, providing something for the choir to sing on Sunday, outshining a rival composer, earning a place in the classical canon, and – not least of all – paying next month's rent. Moreover, a composer could conceivably intend all of these and even more varied outcomes in composing any given piece of music. In terms of explicitness, there is reason to think that composers' intentions are likewise varied. We have all had the experience of performing actions that seemed to us to spring from very definite motives, yet we likewise know what it is to perform actions with motives and purposes that are far less distinct and intelligible to us: we sometimes have a vague idea of what we meant to accomplish, but no more than that. Furthermore, the point at which those intentions take shape is not always at the beginning; instead, it may only become clear during the action itself or even sometime after completion.

As an example, Mozart's compositional process proves to be relatively straightforward, even if not quite as simple as has traditionally been thought. Although there is no denying that Mozart sometimes worked very quickly and without the same degree of painstaking effort characterizing some other composers, recent studies by Ulrich Konrad give us a somewhat different picture than that of the legend.[49] As it turns out, what remains of Mozart's sketches shows us that – like any other composer – Mozart found it necessary to make preliminary sketches, and the fact that he seems to have used an erasable slate in composing tells us considerably more.[50] While a famous story has it that the Violin Sonata in B-flat major (K454) was written in an hour, Konrad points out that Mozart probably spent more than a week working on it. It is also enlightening that Mozart refused to compose without a keyboard at hand, for the traditional view is that he was able to compose everything "in his head." From the sketches, we can see that Mozart often started with a fairly clear idea of what he was aiming at, although the final form of this idea usually varied from its first form and Mozart not infrequently changed his mind along the way.

In contrast to Mozart, Beethoven's compositional process proves to be far more tortuous. For many of his works there are distinct stages, sometimes separated from each other by a year or more. Over the course of eight years, Beethoven composed fourteen different versions of the opening melody of the second movement to his Fifth Symphony, the final version incorporating elements from all of the previous ones. Moreover, he wrote up to twenty different versions of other passages.[51] Beethoven's sketches provide a visual picture of indecision: they are full of passages and even whole pages that have been scratched out,

---

[49] Ulrich Konrad, "Mozart's Sketches," *Early Music* 20 (1992) 119–30.

[50] Most of Mozart's manuscripts were simply thrown away after his death, being judged by his wife Constanze to be worthless.

[51] As part of one of his recordings of the Fifth Symphony, Leonard Bernstein discusses the process that Beethoven went through in composing the Fifth Symphony and provides recorded examples of **how** some alternate versions would have sounded (Sony SXK 47645).

then rewritten only to be crossed out once again (and, not infrequently, again and again). Clearly, the process of selecting the properties that he intended to constitute the work did not stop with just "writing it down." But when did it stop then? It turns out that this is a more difficult question to answer than we might assume: for we tend to expect that it came to an end when, having worked out all of the possibilities and having made up his mind, he wrote up a final version.

Yet, precisely this idea of a "final version" itself poses certain questions, if not for performers at least for musical editors. For, as with many other composers, the "selection process" continued in Beethoven's mind long after what we take to be the "final version." One reason for this was simply the result of finally being able to *hear* his symphonies performed. In the case of the *Eroica*, Beethoven was only certain of what he wanted *after* being able to hear a number of different performances and so able to compare different results. And it is not even possible to say that – having heard and compared – he was finally *certain*. Thus, Barry Cooper, on the basis of extensive study of Beethoven's sketches and manuscripts, concludes that his "compositional activity sometimes continued after one might expect it to have stopped, with Beethoven continuing to add finishing touches as if never fully satisfied with what he had written."[52]

The problem with deciding at what point Beethoven came to a definite decision is that he apparently – at least in some cases – was not fully satisfied and often kept tinkering with his pieces on the day of the performance or even long after a piece had been printed. Furthermore, the changes that he made were not limited to small corrections, for at times he dropped whole movements. Perhaps the best example of this is the last movement of

[52] Barry Cooper, *Beethoven and the Compositional Process* (Oxford: Clarendon Press, 1990) 171.

one of his late string quartets, the B-flat Major Quartet (Op. 130):
Beethoven replaced this with one that was altogether different,
turning the original finale into the *Grosse Fuge* (Op. 133).[53] An
even more interesting case is that of his *Leonora Overture* – or,
more accurately, *Leonore Overtures* I, II, and III, since Beethoven
wrote three different versions. Being unhappy with the first version (Op. 138), he substituted the second (Op. 72a) in the premiere of 1805. Yet, he went on to revise the opera and wrote still a
third version of the overture (Op. 72b) for a performance a year
later. As it turns out, these versions are so different that they can
be performed in the same concert. Are there, then, three different overtures? Or simply three versions of one overture? Here our
intuitions are somewhat conflicting, although most of us would
probably think of the three "versions" as more or less distinct
pieces. The problem, of course, is that there really isn't anything
definite that allows us to make the decision one way or another. We
can appeal to various features of the three versions/overtures in
order to argue that they have "separate" identities – or that they
aren't really so separate after all. The opus numbers are one way
of working out the compromise, although they betray a lingering
indecision.

How much, though, *does* a version need to differ from another
in order to be declared a separate work? Simply put: there are no
clear-cut guidelines here, although our ontological intuitions often reflect our values. If we consider Handel's "borrowing," for instance, we realize that these limits have obviously been construed
differently. Handel could recycle parts of his old compositions
and those of others and turn them into new compositions. And
perhaps the primary reason why at least *he* could do so – without

---

53 While Beethoven may have been pressured into this move by his publisher, a pecuniary motive also may have played a role: in turning the last
   movement into a separate piece of music, he was able to receive royalties
   for two pieces instead of one.

being accused of gross and reprehensible plagiarism – was because the main concern of composers at this point was that of
use. They did not see themselves as creating autonomous works
that would earn them a place in the musical pantheon but, rather,
simply coming up with music that would be suitable for specific
occasions within a specific community. It is primarily a question,
then, of competing values. *We* place a great deal of emphasis on
what we call "originality" precisely because composition today is
guided by the ideal of the autonomous "work" (which needs a
clear-cut identity), not as something that is simply a part of an ongoing musical dialogue. Thus, we would consider Handel guilty
of "plagiarism," for what he did conflicts with our values. We *care*
that works have a distinct identity. Whether we should, of course,
is a very different question.

In any case, Beethoven is by no means a rare exception in
having created multiple versions: many composers have felt the
need to revise their compositions, sometimes so drastically that
they end up seeming to be very different works. For instance,
twenty-five years after its premiere in 1927, Hindemith transformed *Cardillac* from a three-act opera into one of four acts,
substantially changing both its length and general character. So
are there two operas here or merely one? Again, it is difficult to
know how to answer this question. It becomes even more difficult
with an example like Mahler's First Symphony: for, while Mahler
wrote the bulk of it in 1888, not only does it utilize material from
the 1870s but also he revised it more than once, the last version
being published in 1906. Were these revisions simply a matter of
tinkering, we might be tempted to ignore them. But the two later
versions represent very significant improvisations on the first version, and alternatively added and subtracted movements. What,
then, are we to make of this "work"? Should we simply call them
"different" works? Of course, that was not Mahler's inclination.
But, if we take the First Symphony as having a *continuing* identity

between 1888 and 1906, that identity was hardly an *unchanging* one.[54]

How editors of both literary and musical texts have tended to deal with this problem is by way of the idea of the *Fassung letzter Hand* – the final manuscript of the writer or composer. That is, in the case of a composer who has written, say, various preliminary sketches, a first version, and then a revised version (or a number of versions), we simply take the final (that is, chronologically last) version as authoritative. Whereas some performers seeking a historically accurate performance have assumed that the "first" performance is in some sense exemplary, here the assumption is that the last "version" (which, of course, could be the one performed at the *Uraufführung* – the premiere) is authoritative. The idea is, to quote Georg von Dadelsen, that "the last version is always also the best [*die letzte Fassung ist immer auch die beste*]."[55] The assumption here is that the process of composition is one of continual improvement, a kind of hunt in which the composer keeps searching for a solution. In fact, Bernstein speaks of Beethoven as seeking not just the "right notes," but the "right rhythms, the right climaxes, the right harmonies, the right instrumentation."[56] Note how clearly Bernstein is indebted to the Beethoven scholar Heinrich Schenker. What von Dadelsen points out is that Schenker's analyses of Beethoven's works

> assume that in every case the masterworks would have, in the end, been given a form that was definitive, even to the smallest detail. Every note, every nuance of expression indubitably stands in their place. What Schenker intends to show through

---

[54] For more on these kinds of identity problems in Mahler, see Hermann Danuser, *Gustav Mahler und seine Zeit* (Laaber: Laaber Verlag, 1991) 108–19.

[55] Georg von Dadelsen, "Die 'Fassung letzter Hand' in der Musik," *Acta Musicologica* 33 (1956) 7.

[56] Found on Sony SXK 47645.

his analysis is that the Master could only have composed it as it is, and no other way.[57]

Of course, these assumptions (which are far more ideological than musical) reflect the way we think about our musical masterpieces: we assume that, being perfect, "they could not be otherwise."

Yet, this assumption of a process leading to perfection is – at the very least – open to question. Did Beethoven's and Mahler's composing processes only serve to improve their works? While in most cases we might be inclined (and probably even justifiably so) to think that Beethoven enhanced his works through the process of revision and alteration, it is improbable that all of Beethoven's alterations were necessarily for the better. Although it might be difficult to decide either way, many would argue (and perhaps rather heatedly, as I have personally discovered) that, concerning the B-flat Major Quartet, Beethoven should have left well enough alone. Further, Bernstein's assumption that Beethoven somehow found the "exactly right" notes for the opening to the second movement of the Fifth Symphony is dubious at best: even if we could go so far as to argue that Beethoven's compositional process *generally* served to improve his works, we can hardly make the further assumptions that it *always* did or that his pieces ever reached the point at which they could in no way be further improved or that Beethoven ever arrived at what could be described as the "right" notes. Where Bernstein is justified, however, is where he goes on to claim that the composer's job is "to *convey* [my italics] a sense of rightness, a sense that whatever note succeeds the last is the only possible note that can happen at that precise instant." Perhaps we could say that the mark of a fine composer is this ability to *convince*

---

[57] "Die 'Fassung letzter Hand' in der Musik" 7.

us that the work "could not be otherwise." And this is likewise the mark of a fine performer: the ability to convince us (even if only for that particular moment in time) that a specific rendering is the "right" one (and that any other one would simply be inferior).

But what counts as an "improvement"? It seems plausible that at least some of Beethoven's changes served neither to enhance his works nor to detract from them; instead, they may be simply alternatives – each of which might have particular merits and disadvantages, and none of which could be considered as undoubtedly better than any of the others. Why we tend to think of the version Beethoven finally accepted as being obviously superior to others probably has more to do with simply being accustomed to it than with any definite aesthetic superiority. Precisely because of this, it is difficult to come up with a counterexample. Since we are used to the opening of the second movement of Beethoven's Fifth Symphony in the version in which it is normally performed, we are likely to reject as inferior any of the other possibilities that Beethoven entertained. Thus, when Bernstein performs certain alternatives that Beethoven rejected, we are easily persuaded that Beethoven made the right choice. However, as Robert Levin has (I think) convincingly demonstrated, if we take unfinished works of Mozart, for instance, and supply alternative endings (which are unfamiliar to us), it becomes immediately clear that more than one possibility can sound as if it were the "right" solution; and it seems impossible to decide one way or the other.[58] Of course, one *could* argue that, if we only had Mozart's version, we would immediately recognize it as "right"; but such an argument has no basis.

[58] At a public lecture (*"Autograph und Rekonstruktion,"* given at the Staatliche Hochschule für Musik Freiburg in 1991). One can hear Levin's "repair" of the traditional Süssmayr "completion" of Mozart's *Requiem* on Telarc CD-80410 (recorded by the Boston Baroque, with Martin Pearlman conducting).

If composing is the process of selecting, in what sense do musical works reach a kind of completion? What signals the end of the
selection process on the part of the composer? There are at least
two senses in which we can ask this question. First, we usually assume that, at some definite cut-off point, composers in effect say:
"It is finished." However, that is not necessarily the case, and perhaps not even *usually* the case. The realities facing a composer –
particularly one who is financially dependent on churning out a
steady stream of compositions – is that there comes a time where
the compositional process is simply *ended* for what we might term
"nonartistic" reasons, such as deadlines of performance or publication or being too busy with other projects (which effectively
ended the compositional process for Beethoven in many cases),
or simply death. Some composers may perhaps reach a point of
"official completion," but others clearly do not. Likewise, it is not
uncommon for painters, for instance, *never* to reach to a point
at which they consider their paintings to be truly done (which
is often why they will insist on holding on to them). Monroe
Beardsley argues that it may not be the same thing for the *artist*
to be finished as for the *work* to be finished, for artists may feel
that they have done everything possible and still not have the
assurance that a work deserves to be declared finished.[59] But, if
the artist is not finished, can we say the work is truly "finished"?
Shouldn't we rather say that the artist has simply stopped working
on it, leaving the question of its being finished (or not) open?
Such is the case with many of Beethoven's compositions:

> Works that are today so often regarded as perfect masterpieces
> were apparently considered by Beethoven to be full of imperfec-
> tions and in need of sometimes severe revision; these revisions

[59] Monroe C. Beardsley, "On the Creation of Art," in *Art and Philosophy:
Readings in Aesthetics*, ed. W. E. Kennick (New York: St. Martin's Press,
1979) 155–6.

failed to be carried out only because he was too preoccupied
with other matters.[60]

We tend to think of works as being finished in the sense that nothing further could be done to them, but the reality is more often
the case: that they are finished in the sense that the composer
simply has no more time to work on them further. So, properly
speaking, they are not really "finished" at all.

While we distinguish between what counts as a finished work
and an unfinished one, such a distinction is – at least partially, if
not to a great extent – dependent upon the conventions of a given
practice. In certain practices (jazz comes to mind here), such a
distinction would be of relatively little import, assuming it were
made at all. Furthermore, although we rightly make a distinction between Schubert's unfinished symphony and Beethoven's
finished symphonies, perhaps that distinction is not really so distinct. Had Schubert been in need of some ready cash and simply
declared these two movements a two-movement something or
other, *then it would be a finished work*; and we really wouldn't know
the difference. What further complicates such a question is the
existence of intervening versions in certain cases: should each
of these versions themselves be regarded as separate pieces, or
are they no more than variations on a theme? How *do* we differ-
entiate between what we call a fragment and a completed work?
Normally, we do so on the basis of the composer pronouncing
a piece of music to be finished, but clearly there is something
problematic about this. What are we to make of the fact that
Beethoven *himself* thought that some of his works were not yet
finished? Clearly, in some cases we simply ignore what the composer or painter thinks – and call them finished anyway. Perhaps
that is simply the most practical thing to do. Yet, one has a strange

---

[60] *Beethoven and the Compositional Process* 174.

sort of feeling when walking around the Tate Gallery and seeing the canvases of Turner that are labeled "unfinished": for some of them seem not so very different from the finished ones (and one is inclined to wonder exactly how it was decided which ones were finished and which ones were not). In any case, the vicissitudes of life have a way of deciding that something is finished – whether or not the artist is of the same opinion.

There is another sense, though, in which we might say that works are never quite finished, or rather finished only in a restricted sense: for, if composition is a process of selection, how much of a musical work is actually selected? At one point, Ingarden states that in composing a particular piece of music, the various aspects of the composition "have been conceived by the composer as *fully* defined and fixed" (my italics)."[61] To what extent is a composition ever "fully defined"?

As it turns out, the very text from which that quote is taken provides us with a telling example. Ingarden claims that the section "The Musical Work" was first written (in German) in 1928 as an appendix to his text *Das literarische Kunstwerk: Eine Untersuchung aus dem Grenzgebiet der Ontologie, Logik und Literaturwissenschaft* (which he subsequently published in 1931). Yet, before publication, Ingarden decided that *Das literarische Kunstwerk* was already too long, so he *deleted* "The Musical Work" (as well as three other sections) from the text. But then, in 1933, Ingarden decided to translate *a portion* of it from German into Polish with the title "The Problem of the Identity of the Musical Work."[62] Only in 1961 did Ingarden publish the whole of "The Musical Work" (with the three other sections) as part of *Untersuchungen zur Ontologie der*

[61] Roman Ingarden, *The Work of Music and the Problem of Its Identity*, ed. Jean G. Harrell, trans. Adam Czerniawski (Berkeley and Los Angeles: University of California Press, 1986) 116.

[62] "Utwór muzyczny i sprawa jego tożsamości," in *Przeglad Filozoficzny* 36 (1933).

Kunst [*Ontology of the Work of Art*]. Interestingly enough, in his foreword to that text, Ingarden gives a detailed history of his revisions on the three other parts of the text, but makes no mention of any revision of "The Musical Work." One assumes, then, that "The Musical Work" remained unchanged from 1928 to 1961. Yet, the quotation cited at the beginning of this paragraph *only appears in the Polish version*, not in the German version. Ingarden may well be right when he says that he "translated a large part of the essay on "The Musical Work" into Polish," but translation is not *all* that he did. Clearly, there was some revision along the way.[63]

More important, though, not only is this passage from *The Work of Music and the Problem of its Identity* not to be found in *Ontology of the Work of Art*, but Ingarden makes a statement later in *both* texts that can only be read as contradicting that passage.

> Even the most brilliant composer cannot know his work in the whole fullness of its qualification before its performance. He imagines his work only more or less "unclearly," and sometimes he discovers only in the first performance what exactly he has created.[64]

Such an account can hardly fit with the claim that the composer has "fully defined and fixed" the contours of a composition. While it should be obvious that composers usually have certain definite (or at least *reasonably* definite) intentions, it would be impossible for their intentions to encompass all of the details of any given piece. What that means in practice is that

---

[63] *Ontology of the Work of Art* ix. See Ingarden's own description of this convoluted journey, *Ontology of the Work of Art* ix–xi.

[64] Ibid. 113. The version in *The Work of Music and the Problem of Its Identity* (148) reads as follows: "But, strictly speaking, before the performance of his work, even the composer himself does not know the profile in all its qualifications; at best he imagines it more or less precisely *and at times he may merely be guessing at it*" (my italics).

composers are not always sure how their compositions should sound.

An astonishing illustration – although hardly an *admission* – of this lack of certainty is Stravinsky. If ever there were a composer who seemed to be absolutely sure of his intentions (and insisted on them being followed to the letter), it was he; yet, despite his detailed instructions, Stravinsky does not seem to have been quite certain as to what he wanted. Not only do his five recordings of *Le Sacre du Printemps* (*The Rite of Spring*) – made between 1925 and 1961 – differ from one another, they differ from his own score, in terms not merely of tempi but even *notes*.[65] Should the performer take these recordings seriously? Obviously, Stravinsky did. But taking them seriously only complicates the situation. For now the performer is faced with competing sets of "instructions." And the question of which of these represent the composer's *true* intentions remains. Speaking of performing Chopin, Edward Cone nicely captures the dilemma facing performers:

> The performer's first obligation, then, is to the score – but to what score? The autograph or the first printed edition? The composer's hasty manuscript or the presumably more careful copy by a trusted amanuensis? The composer's initial version or his later emendation? The first German edition or the first French edition? An original edition or one supposedly incorporating the composer's instructions to his pupils? Those involved in the attempt to establish a canonic text of Chopin's works face all these decisions.[66]

---

[65] Michael Chanan, *Repeated Takes: A Short History of Recording and Its Effects on Music* (London: Verso, 1995) 123. Note that the problem of differing multiple recordings is likewise to be found with Stravinsky's *L'oiseau de Feu* (*The Firebird Suite*).

[66] Edward T. Cone, "The Pianist as Critic," in *The Practice of Performance: Studies in Musical Interpretation* (Cambridge: Cambridge University Press, 1995) 244.

And those involved in performing Stravinsky face even more complicated decisions.

The problem is that there really is no clear *principle* here by which one may decide. One simply has to make a decision. That is hardly to say that such a decision is whimsical and "anything is permissible." For there are certainly *reasons* that one can give for preferring one "solution" over another. But it is to recognize that performers *too* are part of the "selection" process. That they *too* are important in determining the contours of a given piece of music. And that importance will become far more evident in the next chapter.

An even more remarkable example of composer uncertainty (and thus performer participation in the composing process) can be found in Elliott Carter, as is evident from the comments he made in supervising a rehearsal of his *Duo* for violin and piano.

> Whenever the performers sought guidance on matters of balance and tempo, [Carter's] reply was invariably, "I don't know, let's see . . ." and then he would join them in seeking solutions, as often asking their advice as they his. . . . At the end of the rehearsal he commented that every performance of the *Duo* was very different from every other one, but that "whichever one I'm hearing always seems the best."[67]

While Carter's indecision seems surprising to us, perhaps it is only surprising because we overestimate the ability of the composer to choose and to be sure of what he really wants. Some reflection, however, should show that such an assumption is unwarranted. For instance, when we talk about Beethoven's intentions as being in flux, what we are primarily talking about are his intentions in regard to specific notes and the structure of the composition. Even if were we to say that Beethoven finally reached some

---

[67] Richard Taruskin, "On Letting the Music Speak for Itself," in *Text and Act* 54.

point at which he was certain which notes he wanted, we could hardly infer that Beethoven was certain about how he wanted those notes to be played. In all likelihood, Beethoven had some *general* ideas concerning this, but not necessarily *specific* intentions regarding each and every note. Or he may also have had (like Stravinsky) intentions that kept changing.

Moreover, earlier we noted that intentions can also have various degrees of clarity and indeterminacy: in light of this, a composer could have highly defined intentions concerning particular passages or specific aspects of a piece and yet only indistinct ones (or simply nonexistent ones) concerning other passages and different aspects. Alternatively, a composer might desire to achieve a certain overall musical effect and yet not be certain exactly how to bring this about; or, the specific notes could be clear in the composer's mind, but not the tempo or dynamics (and the composer could well be able to envision playing it various ways). Furthermore, works composed for an ensemble pose a far greater challenge than those for a solo instrument (particularly one which the composer is able to play): while a composer writing piano music, for example, might be able to play a piece through to hear what it sounds like, someone composing choral or orchestral music is simply unable to imagine *all* of the aspects which need to go into a performance. What changes might have Beethoven made had he actually *heard* the Ninth Symphony? In any case, this gives us some idea of the important role that performances play, a subject to which we turn shortly.

From our study of the composing process, we can hardly conclude that composers have no intentions or are always uncertain about them. Rather, it seems that composers usually have some very definite intentions and have often insisted that those intentions be followed. What is at question, though, is how far those intentions extend and how clearly they are intended (that is, to use Husserlian language, whether they are "vague" or "distinct").

A composer may have definite intentions concerning certain aspects of a piece but not necessarily of others. It is even quite possible (as in the case of Carter) that such indeterminacy can be extremely broad. Of course, in such cases of lack of determinacy, the composer may be unaware of it (until, perhaps, the first performance – or perhaps even later). Moreover, we have likewise seen that composers often change their minds over time. Sometimes this is because they begin with certain definite ideas and then change to other definite ideas. Sometimes it is because they begin with few definite ideas and get more along the way. Or perhaps they may start with definite ideas and, upon hearing various performances, become less "certain" of what they want and more open to a wider range of possibilities.

Interestingly enough, however much Hirsch insists on the will of the author (that is, the author's "intentions") as the final determinant of the meaning of a text, he admits precisely the ambiguity of authorial meaning that we have seen all along in this chapter. As he puts it: "An author almost always means more than he is aware of meaning, since he cannot explicitly pay attention to all the aspects of his meaning."[68] And Hirsch complicates this further by saying: "It is not possible to mean what one does not mean, *though it is very possible to mean what one is not conscious of meaning.*"[69] These admissions compromise not only the *ideal* of interpretation as guided by the will or intention of the author but the very *concept* of authorial intention. What is it to "have" a meaning of which one is not conscious? Even if we grant that this makes sense on the basis of a Freudian conception of the unconscious, it is hard to see how an unconscious meaning can be a significant guide to the musical performer, who is faced with practical decisions.

[68] *Validity in Interpretation* 48.
[69] Ibid. 22 (my italics).

Where Hirsch is more plausible is in providing a relatively "wide" conception of determinacy, one that allows for the kinds of indeterminacies that we have already seen and will become even more evident in Chapter 3. Although he is speaking of "verbal" content in the following passage, what he says is applicable to "musical" content.

> Determinacy does not mean definiteness or precision. Undoubtedly, most verbal meanings are imprecise and ambiguous, and to call them such is to acknowledge their determinacy: they are what they are – namely ambiguous and imprecise – and they are not univocal and precise. This is another way of saying that an ambiguous meaning has a boundary like any other verbal meaning, and that one of the frontiers on this boundary is that between ambiguity and univocality.[70]

What does it mean for an ambiguous meaning to have a "boundary"? Isn't the very notion of "boundary" connected to *precision* (that is, "the boundary is here and not over there")? Not necessarily. For, while boundaries can be conceived like steel fences that run along a straight line and do not bend in the wind, they can likewise be thought of as flexible, permeable – and even changing. And I will be arguing for precisely the latter sort of conception of the "boundaries" of a piece of music.

Yet, the ambiguity of composers' intentions is not the only complication facing performers. Not only do those intentions come in varying degrees of precision but they also come with varying degrees of insistence by the composer on *whether* and *how* they should be respected. Concerning the *Hammerklavier Sonata*, in a letter to one of his former students Beethoven actually authorizes switching the order of the Adagio and the Scherzo movements and even goes so far as to sanction dropping the Fugue's introduction, should that be found necessary – what

[70] Ibid. 44–5.

74

could "necessary" possibly mean here? So it would seem that in such a case Beethoven did not see these aspects as essential to a correct performance of the piece.

Perhaps, though, Taruskin goes too far in saying that "once the piece is finished, the composer regards it and relates to it either as a performer if he is one, or else simply as a listener."[71] Taruskin makes this statement on the basis of a distinction between what he calls "composing concerns" and "performing concerns." But, even though this distinction may be valid to a point, I don't think those concerns can be so neatly separated. At least in the practice of classical music, many composers (particularly of the past century or so) have thought that their concerns as composers were – if not equivalent to those of performers – at least not fully separable from them. Practically, that has meant that composers have generally thought that their intentions should be taken seriously. The example of Irving Berlin's comment regarding Fred Astaire that Taruskin gives is telling: "I like him because he doesn't change my songs, or if he does, he changes them for the better." Here Berlin sounds as if he has *both* composing and performing concerns in mind. But perhaps that's an appropriate posture for a composer – holding on to composing concerns ("I like him because he doesn't change my songs") and yet adopting performing concerns ("he changes them for the better").

But what exactly does it mean to take the intentions of a composer (the "composing concerns") *seriously*, especially if they are (to quote Hirsch) "imprecise and ambiguous"? That is the theme of Chapter 3.

---

[71] *Text and Act* 54.

THREE

Performing

The Improvisation of Preservation

WHILE WE HAVE SEEN THAT THE ACTIVITY OF COMPOSING takes place within the framework of a musical discourse or practice, we have concentrated largely on the composer's part of that process. Yet, at least in the discourse of classical music (and even, say, in the composition of jazz tunes), there usually comes a point at which a piece of music takes on written form that gives it a relatively permanent existence, one that often extends far beyond the composer's own existence. But does writing serve *only* to preserve a musical work? What we will see is that making a piece of music publicly available by means of a written score results in both preservation *and* improvisation. And this improvisation affects the very identity of the musical composition.

Unbestimmtheitsstellen and the *Irrelevanzsphäre*

We tend to think of language as a kind of conductor through which thoughts are able to travel from one person to another. Writing takes this a step further, for it provides a lasting link to others in the form of an inscription. Thus, a score – written in a kind of musical language – does not simply provide a way of "remembering" a musical work. It also gives the work a kind of ideal existence, for it takes on a more or less "defined" form and so can be passed on to others. It seems difficult to imagine the discourse of classical music functioning without the use of notation: for scores both serve to define the musical canon and are the main source of access to that canon for musicians. In this respect, classical music would appear to be essentially different from the sort of folk music that is kept alive by way of a "playing" tradition. While such a tradition may well preserve a musical work, it is plausible to assume that a "work" that exists for a long period in such a tradition must inevitably be subject to some degree of improvisational reshaping over time. Within such a tradition, music is passed down from one musician to another; but there is no written reference standing outside of that process. A written score, on the other hand, serves to solidify a work's features and so at least *seems* to provide a kind of absolute standard.

Of course, the centrality of scores in the discourse of classical music also tells us a great deal about our artistic values: for writing not only gives musical works a kind of permanence but also proves an important step in establishing the identity of a work. We have seen that a central ideal of the discourse of classical music is not merely the *preservation* of a musical work but a preservation in which the work is preserved more or less *unchanged*.

Assuming that a composer has declared a given work to be finished (at least as far as the composer is concerned), there is a further complication: for, as some composers have been well aware, the existence of a written score not only serves to preserve a musical work but also effectively enables a work to have a kind of autonomous existence. The existence of a score (or even simply a chart in a fake book) enables a musical work not only to live beyond its author and the historical circumstances in which it arose but also to become part of other musical discourses, perhaps even ones that could be characterized as relatively foreign to that in which a work first arose. Thus, Baroque music has come to be part of what we term classical music, despite the fact that the former substantially differs from the latter. What writing makes possible is both the removal of a piece of music from its original context and the recontextualization of that piece.

Precisely the liberating effect of language creates an inescapable tension. On the one hand, the continued and autonomous existence of their "creations" has been a guiding ideal for many composers of classical music, an ideal that has undoubtedly been fueled by the ideal of artistic immortality. On the other hand, composers have often been reluctant to give up control over their texts and allow them to be truly autonomous. Thus, Stravinsky felt the need to record his pieces (*ad nauseam*) in order to demonstrate to the musical world exactly how they were to be performed. The problem is that, while making one of these ideals possible, it compromises the other. Since scores make a work ideal – in the sense of being available to all – they likewise allow a work to be detached from its composer and open to a wide variety of interpretations.

What exactly is a score able to preserve? While scores clearly provide a way of keeping certain elements of a work from changing, they cannot embody a musical composition in the sense of there being a completely isomorphic relation between the score and what is heard in performance. What, then, are the limits of the score?

To answer this question, it is helpful to consider Ingarden's account of the relation between work, score, and performance. Although Ingarden wants to maintain a clear separation between the work and its written and aural embodiments, the score takes on a highly important role. For the score is not merely incidental: in fact, although he wishes to give the *work itself* priority over scores or performances, the score almost seems to eclipse the work. First, while the score may not be technically the same as the work itself, it is the written notes that serve to "determine mediately how the musical work should be structured and what qualities it should have."[1] As a result, the score "assures the identity of the work."[2] Goodman takes a remarkably similar view, maintaining that the score "has as a primary function the authoritative identification of a work from performance to performance."[3] A second role of the score for Ingarden is as "a system of instructions given implicitly in a kind of shorthand, which dictate how one has to proceed in order to perform the work in question,"[4] a claim with which Goodman would agree. For both Ingarden and Goodman, then, the score serves not only to determine the *identity* of the work but also what counts as a *correct performance* of it. Thus, even though Ingarden talks about the work as if it were some ideal thing, the final court of appeal seems to be that of the score.

However, what we hear in performance is always *much more* than can be indicated in the score, as Ingarden is also well aware. The "imperfection" of musical notation "makes the instructions for performing the work given in this notation incomplete," so that "the work is defined only in a schematic way by the specification of only some determinations."[5] Thus, the score, for Ingarden, can best be described as a kind of *sketch* of what one hears in performance: it prescribes the basic contours of the piece and allows the performer to fill in the rest. Naturally, scores can be more or less defined, as the composer wishes. In some cases, composers provide strict guidelines for the performance of a

---

[1] *Ontology of the Work of Art* 25.
[2] Ibid. 115.
[3] *Languages of Art* 128.
[4] *Ontology of the Work of Art* 115.
[5] *Ontology of the Work of Art* 90.

piece: for example, an exact number of performers, precise bow-
ing directions, a particular type of mute for brass instruments, or
even a different pitch to be used for tuning. Perhaps virtually *any*
aspect of a work could be, at least theoretically, specified; but, in
many cases, such specifications would be only vague at best (and
thus not particularly useful to performers).

Most easily specified are concrete instructions. Of course,
even in terms of designating relatively quantifiable aspects such
as tempo, composers often find it difficult to express exactly
what they want. What are we to make of Beethoven's instructions from the opening of the *C Major Mass*: "Andante con
moto assai vivace quasi allegretto ma non troppo"?[6] How exactly
should that *sound*? Being one of the more controlling composers,
Stravinsky was particularly frustrated by the limits of musical
notation:

> No matter how scrupulously a piece of music may be notated,
> no matter how carefully it may be insured against every possible
> ambiguity through the indications of *tempo*, shading, phrasing,
> accentuation, and so on, it always contains hidden elements that
> defy definition because verbal dialectic is powerless to define
> musical dialectic in its totality.[7]

No doubt, scores do define certain basic contours of a musical work. But, as Ingarden points out, they are always "riddled
with *Unbestimmtheitsstellen*" – that is, places of indeterminacy.[8] In
short, even the most detailed scores significantly "underdeter-
mine" the work. Although scores provide some important bare
facts about a musical work, they only tell us a certain amount

---

[6] Le Huray suggests that here Beethoven was either frustrated by the in-
ability to convey exactly what he wished or else was simply being ironic.
See *Authenticity in Performance: Eighteenth-Century Case Studies* (Cambridge:
Cambridge University Press, 1990) 175.

[7] *Poetics of Music* 127–8.

[8] *Ontology of the Work of Art* 90.

about how a piece of music will *sound*. In short, scores indicate pitches and usually some information concerning how these
should be played, but they do not indicate actual *tones*. Precisely because of this, Ralph Vaughan Williams (perhaps reflecting his own frustrations as a composer) describes the musical
score as "most clumsy and ill-devised." What he claims is that
a score "has about as much to do with music as a time table
has to do with a railway journey."[9] Although Vaughan Williams
might be accused of hyperbole here, there is clearly an important difference between a musical work *as notated* and a musical
work *as heard*. A score might tell us where a musician should
be in terms of precise notes at a given point in the musical
journey – important enough information, as far as it goes – but
the score conveys remarkably little about the musical experience. A score is itself limited in terms of defining the limits of
the musical work. What this means in practice is that a musical work can be interpreted (which is to say "instantiated" or
"embodied") in various ways, none of which necessarily have
any priority over the others.[10] Thus, even if we insist on some
sort of "authenticity" (however that ends up being defined),
there is always a good deal of room left over for the performer's
creativity.

Not only do performers have *room* for improvisation but also
it is *required*: for there can be no performance without filling in these *Unbestimmtheitsstellen*. But, if a performance cannot help but make the score's *Unbestimmtheitsstellen* determinate,

---

9 Ralph Vaughan Williams, "The Letter and the Spirit," in *National Music
and Other Essays* (Oxford: Oxford University Press, 1987) 124.
10 Obviously, I fully agree with Michael Krausz when he says "to insist that
the range of ideally admissible interpretations must always be singular
is to violate an entrenched feature of classical interpretations." See his
"Rightness and Reasons in Musical Interpretation," in *The Interpretation of
Music: Philosophical Essays*, ed. Michael Krausz (Oxford: Clarendon Press,
1993) 87.

then selecting is not merely an aspect of composing but also of *performing*, as Ingarden points out.

> Even in these features of the work that have been recorded with the help of notes, we find a large number of different types of imprecision of determination.... But in the individual performances of the work they must *ipso facto* be eliminated and replaced by sharp, univocally structured determinacies, the selection of which is necessarily left to the talent and discretion of the performer.[11]

Rather than providing complete instructions, scores may not necessarily even tell us exactly what notes to play. Sometimes the way to play a piece "correctly" is by *not following* what the composer has written. A trained musician knows that, on the basis of the style of music, there are times where what the composer has notated should be in effect "disregarded," or at least not taken literally. As an example, in Baroque and Renaissance music a composer may have written particular notes, but the conventions of "following" those notes might be that one turns what stands as a single note into a trill or adds accidentals.

Furthermore, if we consider Mozart's piano concertos, we see that the musical interpreter is required to do far more than reproduce what is there, which the pianist Alfred Brendel describes from his own experience:

> One look at the solo parts of Mozart's piano concertos should be enough to show the Mozart player that his warrant leaves that of a museum curator far behind. Mozart's notation is not complete. Not only do the solo parts lack dynamic markings almost entirely; the very notes to be played – at any rate in the later works that were not made ready for the engraver – require piecing out at times: by filling (when Mozart's manuscript is limited to sketchy indications); by variants (when relatively

---

[11] *Ontology of the Work of Art* 105.

simple themes return several times without Mozart varying them himself); by embellishments (when the player is entrusted with a melodic outline to decorate); by reentry fermata (which are on the dominant and must be connected to the subsequent tonic); and by cadenzas (which lead from the six-four chord in quasi-improvisational fashion to the concluding tutti).

Thus, the performer is required to fill in the gaps and provide embellishments or cadenzas as appropriate. Given these *Unbestimmtheitsstellen*, Brendel concludes that "additions to Mozart's text are in some instances obviously required, in others at least possible."[12] Yet, even if we take a score in which things are far more clearly spelled out – say, a score of Stravinsky – there is still much left to the performer's own discretion.[13] For, far more important than the question of simply *which* notes should be played is that of *how* they should be played. Should the notes be played legato? What sort of attack might be best? How much vibrato should the performer use? Of course, an experienced performer is likely to have a relatively good idea of what to do. Yet, this knowledge comes not from the score but from the performer's experience. A performer is able to translate those notes into sounds on the basis of an acquaintance with a performance practice. Without being steeped in that practice, the notes would communicate little. And these decisions cannot be simply dismissed as unimportant: for it is precisely what is *not* to be found in the score that we often most value. How those

---

[12] Alfred Brendel, *Music Sounded Out* (New York: Farrar Straus Giroux, 1990) 6–7.

[13] As much as he must have hated to admit it, Stravinsky did acknowledge that it is not possible "to convey a complete or lasting conception of style purely by notation. Some elements must always be transmitted by the performer, *bless him.*" See Igor Stravinsky and Robert Craft, *Conversations with Igor Stravinsky* (Berkeley and Los Angeles: University of California Press, 1980) 121 (my italics).

notes are *played* explains why an interpretation by von Karajan or Stokowksi not only *sounds* so radically different from one, say, by Hogwood or Pinnock, but may well have a radically different *effect* on us – and that effect may well cause us to choose one over the other.

If performers cannot help but be improvisers, then where exactly are the limits of this improvisation to be drawn? Such limits vary from piece to piece and era to era. Composers not only give different specifications for their pieces but also different levels of specification. A piece of music can be minimally or considerably more strongly determined. However, there is more to this question than merely differences between particular works: for it clearly depends on what one takes to count as "determinative" not only of a work's identity but of what the performer *must* do. While Ingarden realizes that musical works are not (as he puts it) "wholly univocally determined" in every respect, his way of explaining the difference between the work and what is heard in performance is by way of what he terms an *Irrelevanzsphäre* – a sphere of irrelevance.[14] Although this term does not play an important role in Ingarden's phenomenology, the concept certainly does. What Ingarden means is that the limits of a musical work are somewhat flexible and certain variations in performance are simply irrelevant to the work's identity, for "the work itself remains outside their reach."[15] But exactly what counts as the *work*, the supposedly "unchanging" ideal entity, as opposed to those aspects that are simply irrelevant? Just how broad (or narrow) is this sphere of irrelevance?

[14] *Ontology of the Work of Art* 14, 124–5n11 and *The Work of Music and the Problem of Its Identity* 22–3. As Ingarden himself tells us, this term comes from W. Conrad's "Der ästhetische Gegenstand" in *Zeitschrift für Ästhetik und allgemeine Kunstwissenschaft* 3–4 (1908–9).
[15] *Ontology of the Work of Art* 12 (translation modified).

Stephen Davies defines an authentic performance in terms of being "faithful to the composer's determinative intentions."[16] That definition has at least a *prima facie* plausibility. Yet, what is at issue here is what counts as "determinative" as opposed to something merely "suggested" or simply irrelevant. There are different ways of answering this question. On Goodman's account, the limits of a piece of music are defined primarily in terms of right and wrong notes. Because of this, he cannot help but take what seems to be a rather curious position. On the one hand, as we noted in Chapter 1, for Goodman any performance is disqualified as a "real" performance that has even one wrong note. Yet, on the other hand, he is perfectly willing to say that "performances that comply with the score may differ appreciably in such musical features as tempo, timbre, phrasing, and expressiveness." The reason is because these aspects only affect "the quality of the performance but not the identity of the work." So, on Goodman's account, *only the notes determine the identity of the work.* But Goodman readily admits that "an incorrect performance, though therefore not strictly an instance of a given quartet at all, may nevertheless – either because the changes improve what the composer wrote or because of sensitive interpretation – be better than a correct performance."[17] Thus, there are two criteria here: an ontological one and an aesthetic one. While the first might be compatible with the second, such is not necessarily the case.

Conversely, while Ingarden does not take such a stringent position on wrong notes, his position turns out to be strict in a different sense: for his requirements for correctness extend to how those notes are played. This becomes particularly apparent when Ingarden describes what he terms a "false" performance

---

[16] Stephen Davies, "Authenticity in Musical Performance," in *British Journal of Aesthetics* 27 (1987) 45.

[17] *Languages of Art* 117, 119–20, 185, and 186.

as being "'too fast', 'colorless', 'too loud', etc." Thus, the performance "would have to be quite different in order to render the work 'faithfully'."[18] So Ingarden regards tempi and dynamics as belonging not to the sphere of irrelevance *but to the work itself*. What should be apparent, then, is that the difference between Goodman and Ingarden is not simply one concerning what counts as a "correct" performance. It is also one concerning what counts as the *work*. Whereas Goodman defines the work strictly in terms of the notes, Ingarden thinks that the work is something "more." He never quite spells out what this "more" is, but it obviously goes beyond the bounds of the score: for how could a score indicate an aspect such as tone "color"? On Ingarden's account, *neither* the question of correctness *nor* that of the work's identity can necessarily be resolved simply by consulting the score. But, then, what *else* defines the work?

For his part, Wolterstoff claims that one could follow the score and still not actually perform the work:

> One might in every detail follow the specifications for correct occurrence found in (some correct copy of) the score for a work and yet not perform the work. For often the specifications for correct occurrence that composers give in scores are incomplete for ensuring that those who follow them will produce occurrences, let alone correct occurrences, of the work.

As he goes on to add, "many things go presupposed rather than specified."[19] Again, what constitutes the work must be the properties in the score *plus something else*. But what is this something else? Although Wolterstorff never fully spells this out, he gives us some examples. He claims, for instance, that a failure to perform the work may be because one has not performed the work

---

[18] *Ontology of the Work of Art* 13.
[19] *Works and Worlds of Art* 75.

on the instruments that the composer would have presupposed (whether the composer needs to have *specified* those instruments is something that Wolterstorff does not address) or by not following the practice traditions associated with those instruments. In any case, for Ingarden and Wolterstorff (but *not* Goodman – or at least not apparently), there is obviously something necessary both to the work and to a correct performance of it that extends *beyond* the score.

However, if an appeal to the score may be necessary but not *sufficient*, then what is to count as the final court of appeal? The problem is that, if a piece of music really is an ideal entity that is only known by way of the score and the performance, then we don't have a direct contact with the work per se. So the final court of appeal cannot be simply the ideal object itself. As Davies has acknowledged:

> We come to know the work through its performances. We abstract the work from its instances, stripping away from its performances those of their properties that are artistically irrelevant and then stripping away those artistically relevant properties that are properties of the performance but not properties of the work.[20]

But here we come to the very nub of the issue: for how do we distinguish between that which is "irrelevant" and that which is "relevant"? We are back to the problem of Ingarden's *Irrelevanzsphäre*.

[20] Stephen Davies, "The Ontology of Musical Works and the Authenticity of their Performances," *Noûs* 25 (1991) 28–9. Davies himself illustrates this problem when, in criticizing the view of Michael Krausz, he admits that "the work goes beyond the score, in that it presupposes a performance practice." Yet, if the contours of the work are constituted not *merely* by the score but also the performance practice (which is neither uniform nor static), can the work's identity be fully determined? See Stephen Davies, *Musical Works and Performances: A Philosophical Exploration* (Oxford: Clarendon Press, 2001) 111n13.

Davies goes on to admit that "one can distinguish the irrelevant from the relevant properties only in terms of a theory which establishes criteria for relevance."[21] But to what *theory* can we (or *ought* we) appeal? What complicates this question is that each of these theorists – either explicitly or implicitly – take their theories as being reflective of the way in which we *think* about musical works, and this is why they tend to appeal to our intuitions. Thus, we can only conclude that our "intuitions" on the matter do not necessarily agree, even regarding works that are part of the discourse of classical music. The line, then, that separates the work and the *Irrelevanzsphäre* does not seem to be something that can be clearly drawn, as recent debates over authenticity among both musicologists and philosophers have made all too apparent.

Having said that, there is no question that a given musical practice *does* provide quite useful and often even reasonably explicit guidelines for making decisions. If we are playing Beethoven, then the constraints of classical music would seem to suggest that we follow the notes as given in the score, as well as the instructions for dynamics that accompany it (assuming that those instructions are actually those of Beethoven, as opposed to some overzealous editor who added them along the way). But, even then, how seriously are we to take these? Davies claims, for instance, that metronome markings are "nondeterminative"; that is, they "have the status of recommendations" and so can be adjusted to suit particular performances.[22] He goes on to suggest that in any given era there are general conventions as to which determinations of a musical score are determinative and which are nondeterminative. Thus, performers seeking to be historically accurate need simply consult the appropriate conventions

[21] Ibid. 29.
[22] "Authenticity in Musical Performance" 43.

of the day when performing pieces of another era. Davies's suggestion sounds perfectly reasonable, yet we have seen that what falls under the heading of "determinative" even in one's *own* era is not always clear. *Beethoven* seems to have regarded his metronome markings as "determinative." Yet, performers today routinely disregard them. And it is difficult to imagine Stravinsky thinking of *any* of his markings as *mere* recommendations. Note that in a review of three versions of *Le Sacre du Printemps* the *very* first thing he notes about von Karajan's performance is that "a *ritardando* has been substituted for the written *accelerando* in measures 5–6."[23] It is clear that Stravinsky is not pleased.

Yet, there is a further problem here: for, once we recognize that musical works *have a history*, then the situation becomes more complex. This complexity becomes particularly clear in regard to Baroque music. *We* may expect an historically authentic performance to mirror the original performance conditions; but the very notion of a historically authentic performance is *ours*. Transferring it back to Baroque music may result in intriguing performances, but it is anachronistic. We will consider this problem in more detail in the following section. But what about classical music (in the narrow sense)? Clearly, composers such as Beethoven had a much stricter sense of what they expected of performers and they composed their works accordingly. On the other hand, although the ideal of *Werktreue* has guided classical music for approximately the last two centuries, only in the last half of the previous century has that ideal come to be defined in such literal terms. For example, note what Vaughan Williams

---

[23] Igor Stravinsky and Robert Craft, *Retrospectives and Conclusions* (New York: Alfred A. Knopf, 1969) 123. Of course, coming from Stravinsky, such a criticism of von Karajan comes as no surprise (nor does "too bland, well-blended, sustained"). Stravinsky ends his review with this pronouncement: "None of the three performances [by von Karajan, Boulez, and Kpaøt] is good enough to be preserved."

(clearly someone who comes long *after* the beginning of the Classical era) writes in his entry on conducting that appeared (early in the twentieth century) in the second edition of *Grove's Dictionary of Music and Musicians*:

> Together with this duty [of conducting] goes the responsibility of making certain alterations in the score of well-known works, such as Wagner's famous emendations in the Choral Symphony... or the almost universal substitution of a bass clarinet for a bassoon in a certain passage in Tchaikovsky's sixth symphony. It is a conductor's duty to know of these alterations, and to settle whether he will adhere to the original score or not.[24]

To settle whether he will adhere to the original score or not? Such a question seems odd – *to us.* For we tend to view such changes as being more than merely "irrelevant." In short, they are for us not part of the *Irrelevanzsphäre.* Yet, it would be hard to argue that Vaughan Williams represents a view that is somehow less authentic than ours, for it *too* is representative of a historic era. In the eighteenth, nineteenth, and early twentieth centuries, it was common for conductors to make such changes.[25] And it could easily be argued that it is actually more representative of Beethoven's own sense of *Werktreue* than our decidedly more literal – or fundamentalistic – one. What we tend to forget is that each of these represents different – but valid – traditions.

So the performer must *choose.* Whereas Francis Sparshott claims that a score "can be played straight, but that is not the only thing that can be done with it," Morris Grossman rightly asks: "What is it 'to play a score straight'? A synthesizer might do

---

[24] *National Music* 278–9.
[25] The authors of "performing practice" in *The New Grove Dictionary of Music and Musicians*, 2nd ed., ed. Stanley Sadie (London: Macmillan, 2001) note the difference between the first and second halves of the twentieth century.

this.... But a performer is incapable of having 'nothing in head or hand'."[26] Yet, could even a synthesizer really play something any more "straight" than a performer? As it turns out, synthesizers are programmed by *someone* using some sort of standard; and, whatever standard is used, it can only be defined as "straight" to a degree. Quite unwittingly, Andrew Porter describes the situation perfectly when he speaks of "Mozart productions that people of my age grew up with" as being 'straightforward'."[27] "Straightforward" is constituted by the norm of a given performance tradition.

But, rather than simplifying things, the recognition of the centrality of a performance tradition in interpretation actually serves to complicate them, since performance traditions are *themselves* constantly changing. For example, whereas only twenty or thirty years ago "straight" still meant Solti or Szell (which, in terms of musical style, translates into turn-of-the-century Vienna), more recently it has come to mean something like "historically accurate" (although the pendulum at the moment seems to be swinging back in the Solti sort of direction). So which way of treating the composer's score is more *authentic*? The problem is that the answer cannot be decided by simply examining the phenomena, for it is precisely a question of how to interpret the phenomena. Nor can it be merely a question of setting the piece back in its original context, for the very fact that musical works have an extended life means that they often have already existed in a whole variety of contexts and the original isn't obviously the *best* one. Given the current predilection for historical authenticity, we may think that Bach's version is more authentic. But that is far from clear.

[26] Francis Sparshott, "Aesthetics of Music: Limits and Grounds" 82 and Morris Grossman, "Performance and Obligation" 262, both in *What is Music?*
[27] Andrew Porter, "Mozart on the Modern Stage," *Early Music* 20 (1992) 133.

The Improvisation of Preservation

What do we make of a performer like Jorge Bolet who changes passages in Chopin because he likes his version better? While it is probably a safe assumption that the changes made by a beginning piano student would have little chance of improving Chopin, the changes of a seasoned performer just might (although it seems difficult to know just how to define "better" here). But let's take this a bit further. Suppose, for instance, that a noted Beethoven performer were to perform the *Hammerklavier Sonata* (Op. 106) on a modern Steinway: in what sense would this represent a distortion of the piece? There is no question that Beethoven "designed" it for the Broadwood piano that he had just been sent that same year (1818); and there is also no question that, while the Broadwood is clearly an early version of a *piano*, it is markedly different from a Steinway of today. What pleased Beethoven so much about the Broadwood was that he could play it with great force, as was his style of playing. So would Beethoven prefer the greater forcefulness of the concert grand of today, or the greater expressive capacities of the old Broadwood? Suppose, furthermore, that our performer actually took Beethoven at his word and switched the Adagio and Scherzo around and even omitted the Fugue's introduction: in what sense would she be "distorting" the essence of the *Hammerklavier Sonata?* Despite the fact that Beethoven thought that such changes would be permissible, I suspect many of us would consider them unacceptable. Yet, what if our performer were to go so far as to alter not only the dynamic markings (something that Beethoven's own student Czerny did without batting an eye) but even perhaps certain notes (again a practice that was not foreign to Czerny, who used to add ornaments to Beethoven's pieces whenever it suited his fancy)?

Would we be convinced by the explanation that these changes provided a different way of hearing the work (let alone by the explanation that they simply "sounded better")? Clearly, many concertgoers of today would have significant reservations (assuming, that is, they were able to hear the difference, for few people in the audience would actually know that they were hearing Beethoven "doctored-up"). And what if our performer were to reply by claiming that precisely these sorts of changes would have been perfectly acceptable in the not-so-distant history of the practice of classical music (say, in the day of Chopin)? Or, conversely: what if our performer's defense were that both Baroque performers and jazz performers have been allowed such liberties? Most likely our response would be that these changes go beyond the *Irrelevanzsphäre*.

Would that really answer the question, though? What is presupposed here is that, whereas such improvisation would be fine in jazz, it is "out of place" in classical music (or at least in "classical music" as defined by us in the twenty-first century). I take it that the reason we would give for such a view is that improvisation is part of jazz practice and not part of the practice of classical music. Such seems to be a right answer – as far as it goes. But the answer that classical composers did not intend for their pieces to be improvised on (in a Baroque or jazz sense) and that jazz composers do won't quite do. Not all composers of what are now recognized as jazz "standards" intended for their music to be improvised on. George Gershwin did not object to his tunes being improvised on; but his brother Ira, who wrote the lyrics to most of George's tunes, very explicitly *did*. While George was enthralled with Art Tatum's improvisations on his tunes (and Tatum could take *one* Gershwin tune and improvise on it for close to an hour), Ira maintained that "Tatum should be given a ticket for speeding"; and he had a similar reaction to how vocalists such as Sarah Vaughan treated his lyrics.[28] We noted in the last chapter that Irving Berlin was likewise uncomfortable with people changing his songs. But neither of these reservations has given jazz

[28] Notes to "The Gershwin Connection."

musicians the slightest pause from improvising on Gershwin and Berlin tunes. Nor did the vehement protestations of Couperin (that we noted in Chapter 1) necessarily stop musicians from improvising on his music.

So why do we feel comfortable going against the composer's intentions in one case and not in another? I suspect the answer would end up being either something to the effect that the intentions of composers of popular tunes do not really matter or else some sort of version of the Schenkerian belief that composers of classical music have found just the "right" solution. And one cannot help but suspect that part of the reason that we cling to the ideal of *Werktreue* is because, in the end, we subscribe to at least something akin to Schenker's assumption that the great composer *really does know best.*

But to what extent *should* the performer follow the instructions of the composer "to the letter"? And *which* of those instructions are truly binding? We have seen that Hirsch takes the author's intentions to be the ultimate defining factor of textual meaning. So it seems logical to assume that Hirsch would think that composer's intentions should be strictly obeyed. Note that Hirsch's position is in direct response to W. K. Wimsatt and Monroe Beardsley, who argue that the meaning of a text is not equivalent to what the author intended.[29] They give various reasons for their position, but the primary one is relatively straightforward: whereas a text is something open to public scrutiny, the author's intentions are not. So it is not surprising that Beardsley, when speaking specifically of composer's intentions, claims that they "do not play any role in decisions about how scores ... are to be performed."[30]

[29] W. K. Wimsatt, Jr. and Monroe C. Beardsley, "The Intentional Fallacy," in W. K. Wimsatt, Jr., *The Verbal Icon: Studies in the Meaning of Poetry* (Lexington: University of Kentucky Press, 1954) 3–18.

[30] Monroe C. Beardsley, *Aesthetics: Problems in the Philosophy of Criticism* (New York: Harcourt, Brace & World, 1958) 24.

And this claim is meant to be both *descriptive* (what performers actually do) and *prescriptive* (what performers ought to do). Although Beardsley acknowledges that some performers do follow the composer's intention, he concludes that most do not (and, writing in 1958, that conclusion may have reflected actual practice more closely than it does today). But clearly performers generally *do* follow composer's instructions (in fact, more so today than in 1958). So ought they? Such a question turns out to be central to the restoration of "early music."

Restoring Early Music

Although the "authenticity movement" or "historical performance movement" has become less noticeable in this century, it has hardly disappeared. Indeed, one can argue that the debate that it spawned has died down precisely because many of the assumptions of early music performers have become *mainstream* assumptions. In any case, the very idea that performances *ought* to be (as well as *can be*) historically "authentic" provides a useful test case for my thesis that performers are actually improvisers. Nowhere is the ideal of historic authenticity better expressed than by Nikolaus Harnoncourt when he writes:

> Today we are prepared to accept only the composition itself as our source...we must attempt to hear and play the masterpieces of Bach as if they had never been interpreted, as if they had never been shaped or distorted in performance...we must approach the great masterpieces by pushing aside the lush growth of traditional experience and interpretation, and once again begin from the beginning.[31]

[31] Nikolaus Harnoncourt, *The Musical Dialogue: Thoughts on Monteverdi, Bach and Mozart*, trans. Mary O'Neill (Portland, Ore.: Amadeus Press, 1989) 44.

"Beginning from the beginning" is hardly a new philosophical motif. Descartes may be its quintessential flag bearer, but it is a basic presupposition of modernity. Yet, the idea of returning to the *musical* "things themselves" [*die Sachen selbst*] and of somehow ridding oneself of all musical prejudices (i.e., "the lush growth of traditional experience and interpretation") is a remarkably new phenomenon. The concern of such performers as Harnoncourt is that, while the tradition has transmitted the past, it has done so in a sedimented and thus altered form.

Yet, this ideal itself raises a plethora of problems. First, what would it mean to return to musical origins? Harnoncourt claims to be searching for "the composition itself," something undistorted by the intervening tradition. But is this some original *sound*? Or is it an original musical *effect*? Or is it a kind of musical *meaning*? Second, in what sense can the composition "itself" be separated from the musical tradition? Third, even if we ignore what musicians would see as practical performance questions, how do we choose one performance possibility over another? Fourth, to what extent can twentieth-century performances reflect those of the past? Finally, are we truly interested in *purely* authentic performances? Clearly these questions are not merely musical but deeply philosophical in nature: for at stake is not merely the question of what constitutes "the composition itself" but also how we relate to the musical past.

Before we can address these questions, though, we need to make an important distinction. The historical awareness of musicians today represents both a change in the perceived immediacy between a work's origins and its subsequent performances and a significant conceptual shift. As we noted in Chapter 1, throughout most of the history of Western music, performances were generally of music by *living* composers, which meant that most compositions were remarkably short-lived. The concern for historical authenticity could arise only in a context in which certain compositions have a long life. Just as important, though, the ideal of historical authenticity represents a crucial conceptual change. While *we* take a historical awareness for granted, such an awareness would have been far too self-conscious for performers of even the relatively recent past, who would have simply followed the general conventions of their time. Only comparatively recently (that is, in the last half century) have performers become historically conscious to the extent of, say, using one performance style for Bach and another for Brahms.

Behind this parallel shift in thought and practice is the realization of a rupture in the musical tradition. Dahlhaus speaks of this change in terms of the move from an attitude that he terms "tradition" to that of "restoration." Whereas "tradition presupposes seamless continuity," restoration "is an attempt to renew contact with a tradition that has been interrupted or has atrophied.... And it is this element of restoration, not merely distance in time, that determines whether or not a work is to be considered 'early music'."[32] The distinction Dahlhaus draws here helps to explain why even comparatively "recent" works could be considered early music: the temporal distance denoted by speaking of music as "early" is not one measured so much in terms of years but in terms of perceived *contact*.[33] Often these coincide, so that "old" music is likewise "early."

What is remarkable is how quickly this change has come about. To provide an example of the divide between restoration and tradition, Dahlhaus contrasts Mendelssohn's revival of Bach's *St. Matthew Passion* in 1829 with our relation to Beethoven's

---

[32] Carl Dahlhaus, *Foundations of Music History*, trans. J. B. Robinson (Cambridge: Cambridge University Press, 1983) 69.

[33] Theoretically, then, it is possible to imagine a situation in which relatively recent music (say, recently discovered, previously unperformed avant-garde music from the 1960s) would – on Dahlhaus's definition – qualify for us today as "early."

symphonies: whereas Bach was already "early music" even in Mendelssohn's time, Dahlhaus feels confident enough to assert that today we remain connected to Beethoven because of the continuity of the performing tradition. Until only recently, the standard view was that there exists a fundamental difference in our relationship to works composed before 1750 and to those afterward – the former being separated from us by a kind of historical rupture, the latter being connected by a kind of musical apostolic succession in which the performance tradition has been handed down unchanged.[34]

Here we can turn to our earlier list of questions. To begin, what does it mean to "regain contact" with a work's origins. The possibility of returning to musical works in their original form is dependent on two principal issues: (1) the sort of existence that the work of music has and (2) the connection of musical works to the tradition that has passed them down to us. Precisely such questions – even if not directly concerning musical works – are at the heart of Husserl's essay *The Origin of Geometry*.[35] While there is no reason to think that Husserl had any concern for early music, it is the problem of a loss of contact with origins that motivates his investigation.

On Husserl's view, geometry is a tradition that has been developed by each generation building on the insights of the last. Clearly, this would likewise apply to music and musical works. But what allows a tradition to build on itself? Somehow the insights of those in the past, whether mathematicians or musicians, need

---

[34] This assumption of an unbroken continuity has itself come to be questioned. See the remarkable difference between *The New Grove Dictionary of Music*, ed. Stanley Sadie (London: Macmillan, 1980) and *The New Grove Dictionary of Musical Instruments*, ed. Stanley Sadie (1984), s.v. "Performing practice."

[35] *The Origin of Geometry* is an appendix to *The Crisis of European Sciences and Transcendental Phenomenology* 353–78.

to become available to others – both present and future – or else they would simply die out. We have already seen that Husserl thinks we can "encapsulate" an insight that can be passed on to posterity. So "tradition" is partly a composite of idealities that place an original insight on deposit in such a way that we can always return to it.[36] However, this permanence is bought at a price. Not only does writing make possible performance variations, it also (and inevitably) entails the possibility of a loss of contact with the original intention.

But how does all of this apply to musical works? Musical scores can be affected by their subsequent existence – by what Harnoncourt calls the "lush growth of traditional experience" and what Husserl terms *sedimentation*.[37] So "sedimentation" is simply the history (and sometimes a very *long* history) of the improvisation on a musical work that we call a "performance tradition." Still, Husserl assures us that "desedimentation" is always possible – the original meanings of ideal objects (whether geometric theorems or symphonies) can always be (to use his term) "reactivated." For Harnoncourt, in order for "reactivation" to take place, "all questions must be raised anew, with only Bach's score itself accepted as the crystallization of a timeless work of art in a time-linked form of expression."[38] And what is this "work itself" for Harnoncourt? Interestingly enough, it turns out to be Bach's *score* – that "crystallization of a timeless work." Yet, this "crystallized" work is inevitably linked to time. By making written language a crucial step of the process in which idealities are formed, ideal objects must, at least to some

---

[36] Ibid. 358. Also see Edmund Husserl's *Origin of Geometry: An Introduction* 27.

[37] Reinhard Goebel (the conductor of Musica Antiqua Köln) uses the term "patina" when speaking of the incrustation of years of performance practice. See his notes to Archiv 423 116-2 ST.

[38] *The Musical Dialogue* 44.

degree, become inextricably linked with actual language. Thus, although writing (or "scoring") provides the way to remove an ideal object from specific cultural and temporal confines, as a material inscription, writing likewise inherently entails a close connection with the real world.

This, in turn, poses a problem for Husserl's distinction between "bound" and "free" idealities (which we noted in Chapter 1). Whereas Husserl defines free idealities as those that have no real connection to temporality, bound idealities are those that arise out of yet remain in some way still connected to a particular context. But Husserl's reconnection of ideal objects to factual reality means that even the most "free" of ideal objects – those that can readily transcend cultural and historical boundaries – turn out to be "bound" in the sense of being dependent on their textuality. This aspect is particularly important for the discourse of classical music. At least for music of the last few centuries, the score has functioned as the principal way of passing on musical compositions. Even if we first *hear* a piece, if we wish to play it ourselves, we normally turn to a written text. Practically, the written inscription takes precedence over the aural embodiment. Precisely because of the textuality of a musical work in the discourse of classical music, the score's existence – and, indirectly, the existence of the musical work itself – is always threatened: for "the graphic sign, the guarantee of Objectivity, can also *in fact* be destroyed . . . and nothing can definitively protect inscription from this."[39] Scores can be mutilated or simply lost; and music history is replete with examples. Had not Mozart's widow, for example, happened to think that she might be able to make some money off the manuscripts her husband had left cluttering the house, there would be considerably less in the Mozart repertoire today. Still,

[39] Edmund Husserl's *Origin of Geometry* 94.

musicologists estimate that she burned as many as three thousand pages.

Perhaps the most obvious textual difficulty faced by the performer of early music is simply to find a text that accurately reflects the composition in its original form – that is, in its *Ursprung*. The search, then, is for an *Urtext*. But what is an *Urtext*? Walter Emery suggests that "an 'original text' [*Urtext*] represents, as a rule, not what the composer wrote, but an editor's theory about what the composer *meant to write*."[40] Even if we have an autograph text, Wolterstorff argues that editors of musical texts "try to revise the autograph score received from the composer in such a way that it signifies what the composer *would* have signified, had he made no mistakes in his use of the notation." While Wolterstorff realizes that this inevitably means appealing to a composer's intentions, he characterizes such an appeal as "minimal and innocuous": for it is "no more questionable an appeal to intention than what takes place when a publisher corrects the mistakes in the manuscript that a critic submits. . . . We do not appeal to what he *intended* to select. We appeal to what he *did* select."[41]

The idea here is that editing involves appealing not directly to an author's mental intentions but to the intentions that actually made it onto the page. Of course, there is the problem of deciding what counts as a *mistake* or something that needs to be "corrected." This may be more complicated than Wolterstorff suggests: for, while both musical and literary texts may present us with variant readings, at least the conventions of both spelling and word order represent a degree of standardization that is not found to anything like the same extent in music. What makes

---

[40] Walter Emery, *Editions and Musicians* (London: Novello, 1957) 39 (my italics).

[41] *Works and Worlds of Art* 69 (Wolterstorff's italics).

musical texts more complicated is that, while particular notes (or chords or even whole measures and passages) may not seem to "fit," we have fewer conventions to fall back on. Did the composer mean to create (what at least to us sounds like) a kind of dissonance here? True, we may be able to argue – on the basis of what the composer did select in a particular piece or else in other pieces – that this is out of keeping with the composer's usual style. But establishing conclusively that it is truly a "mistake" may not be possible in certain cases. Not only is this problematic in regard to twentieth-century music – which often is explicitly written to stretch or question conventions – it is also problematic in regard to Medieval or Renaissance music. It was not atypical for composers of those eras to create what sometimes seems (to us) to be inexplicable dissonances.

While it is easy to *overplay* the role of the editor, certainly there have been editors who have significantly shaped the contours of a musical work. Note that Carl Czerny thought nothing of adding all sorts of markings and even notes to his influential 1838 edition of Bach's preludes and fugues. In contrast, we see ourselves as much more sensitive to the ideal of historical purity. Yet, our age is no less involved in improvising on the past: whereas the Victorians had no problems bringing the lyrics of music of the past into line with their more prim sensibilities,[42] we think nothing of bringing religious music into line with current thought by removing infelicitous words or phrases (often gender-exclusive ones) and replacing them with what we would consider to be more neutral ones. Such editing tells us a good deal about our *own* values: we may claim to seek nothing other than the pure *Urtext*, but that doesn't mean we won't improvise on the text to

---

[42] Such as changing "from virgin's womb" to the more discreet "from virgin pure." See Philip Brett, "Text, Context, and the Early Music Editor," in *Authenticity and Early Music*, ed. Nicholas Kenyon (Oxford: Oxford University Press, 1988) 93.

accommodate our sensibilities. Such improvisation is not necessarily inappropriate. But we need to recognize it for what it is – an
improvisation on the past that brings the past more in line with
the present. Of course, historians do this whenever they write history and religious scholars do this whenever they translate sacred
texts. In both cases, it is a kind of preserving by improvisation.
Precisely this kind of improvisatory movement constitutes the
very structure of restoration.

When Husserl speaks of returning to "the submerged original
beginnings of geometry," he is referring to the essential core
standing behind the layers of sedimentation.[43] But what is this
essential core that the performer is supposed to reactivate?

Randall Dipert makes a distinction between low-level, middle-
level, and high-level intentions that is helpful in thinking about
this question.[44] Low-level intentions concern such aspects as instruments used and fingering specified; middle-level intentions
have to do with the sound at which the composer aims; and
high-level intentions can be defined in terms of the effect(s) on
the audience, such as a certain emotional response or the purposes a composer might have in composing a particular piece.
To relate this hierarchy to a common distinction used among
interpreters of many sorts of texts, we could say that low-level
and middle-level intentions constitute the "letter" and high-level
intentions constitute the "spirit." Given this ranking – all things
being equal – it would at least *seem* that the higher intentions take
precedence. Of course, one might argue that – in the best of all
possible worlds – there would be no need to choose. An "ideal
performance," then, would be one in which all three could be
instantiated – equally.

---

[43] *The Crisis of European Sciences* 354.
[44] Randall Dipert, "The Composer's Intentions: An Examination of their
Relevance for Performance," *Musical Quarterly* 66:2 (1980) 206–8.

In previous centuries (that is, up until the middle of the twentieth century), it seems safe to say that performers were generally more concerned with being true to the *spirit* of a piece; that is, they assumed that composers had usually had certain overriding aims in composing certain works and so had tended to view the task of the performer as being primarily concerned with realizing these. No doubt, this is what the early music performer Wanda Landowska expresses in speaking of knowing "what Mozart means when he writes in D major or what Bach wishes to express when he uses the key of E flat major." Thus, the aim of performance was that of expressing a certain feeling or whatever it is that "Bach wishes to express." Here we have a rather different candidate for *Werktreue*, one defined not in terms of notes or instruments used but *effect* or *content to be conveyed*. What might sound callous or disrespectful – such as when Landowska says, "Little do I care if, to attain the proper effect, I use means that were not exactly those available to Bach" – turns out to be a different way of expressing respect, one that can only be understood in light of this conception of musical interpretation as being primarily concerned with the higher purposes of a composer, rather than with the producing of specific sounds.[45]

It is precisely this conception of *Werktreue* behind the justification given by performers (or arrangers or transcribers) that musical pieces needed to be "modernized." Harnoncourt derisively describes such performances by saying: "There was no dutiful feeling that Bach's works should be performed as he had intended. Instead, an attempt was made to 'purify' the baroque compositions, which were generally regarded as 'bewigged' and old-fashioned."[46] Such was also the motive behind

[45] Wanda Landowska, *Landowska on Music*, ed. Denise Restout (New York: Stein and Day, 1964) 406 and 356.
[46] *The Musical Dialogue* 43.

Mozart's reworking of Handel's *Messiah,* a piece that Mozart considered "dated." Whether one agrees with this motive, of course,
is one thing. But it is crucial to realize that Mozart's aim was
to make Handel speak to a new audience. Mendelssohn had no
qualms about taking "liberties" with Bach's *St. Matthew Passion* for
the same reason. He removed a third of the piece (assuming the
audience would not be patient enough to sit through the entire
thing), made severe revisions in scoring and solo parts, and used
158 voices and a large orchestra. Despite all this, he made his
own claim to *Werktreue.*[47]

So how should one define *Werktreue*? For Harnoncourt,
Mendelssohn's performances were unquestionably *not* true to
Bach's instructions, since the *St. Matthew Passion* was hardly presented as *written.* In effect, Mendelssohn altered what he would
have seen as incidental or insignificant *precisely to get back to the core
of what Bach originally intended*: a certain effect that the *St. Matthew
Passion* was to produce on listeners. Of course, the ideal of "realizing what the composer hoped to achieve" is actually a much
more *difficult* ideal than "playing the notes he wanted played."
While it is relatively easy to discern what Bach hoped to achieve
with the *St. Matthew Passion* (something along the lines of having people "moved" spiritually), it seems much more difficult to
know (to quote Landowska) "what Mozart means when he writes
in D major." True, we often have at least *some* conception of what
a composer intends in a particular piece (and perhaps even a
very *good* idea) by way of what has been notated – even without
unmediated access to the "thought processes" of the composer.
Without knowing the title, we would likely not be able to guess
that Handel's *Music for the Royal Fireworks* was designed specifically

[47] "It has always been a rule for me to leave these works absolutely as they
were written, and I have often quarreled with those who did not." Quoted
in Harry Haskell, *The Early Music Revival: A History* (London: Thames and
Hudson, 1988) 15–16, 199n11.

for a fireworks display; but it would be hard to miss the fact that it was devised to communicate a festive mood.

Perhaps the real challenge is not so much knowing but *doing* – particularly when it is a question of taking a piece of music from the past and attempting to make it speak to the present. Suppose a composer did happen to leave what would seem to be an ingenuous and detailed explanation of what the piece was to achieve, in which the spirit of the piece was described in great detail: how would the performer translate this into *musical sound*? It seems safe to say that *even in that situation* performers would still not necessarily agree as to how a piece should sound. Something like "fidelity to the spirit" is, no doubt, an important measure of performance success. But there is no clear standard by which to measure it. It is easy to understand, then, why early music performers have rejected faithfulness to the spirit in favor of something more easily quantified: the composition's letter. Speaking of the end of the "romantic" performance tradition, Brendel astutely notes that "the loss of self-confidence was often followed by a rigid faith in the letter."[48]

Yet, how well does using the letter as our standard fare? To see why this aspiration itself poses a problem, we need to return to the distinction Husserl makes between free and bound idealities. Not only are musical works "bound" to empirical reality by way of writing, they also are bound as products of a particular time and culture. Precisely the recognition of this has been a key impetus behind the desire for period performances. Part of reading a score is reading "between the lines," knowing what sorts of things a composer would have taken for granted given the performance tradition of the time, and so would never even have thought of mentioning.

[48] Alfred Brendel, *Musical Thoughts and Afterthoughts* (Princeton, N.J.: Princeton University Press, 1977) 24.

To fulfill the "letter" of a composer's intention, performers would then need to concentrate on such aspects as the instruments specified, the way those instruments are to be played, and the way the composer would want the piece to sound. The history of musical notation can be roughly generalized as the history of increasing precision. Whereas modern composers tend to specify many details of performance, such is not necessarily the case in earlier music. In Medieval and Renaissance music, for instance, we are not always certain exactly what instruments were used, how such instruments sounded, or even the extent to which instruments were used (if at all). There is a further question, though: even if we were to confine ourselves to intentions concerning such specifics as sound and instruments, which of these should take precedence? Was the composer aiming at a particular sound, so that the instruments are only a means to that sound? Or is there some sense in which using period instruments actually makes the performance more authentic? Levinson argues that "a performance matching the *sound* of an ideal contemporary (and thus, presumably, authentic) performance is not authentic unless this match is brought about through the offices of the *same performance means or instrumental forces* as were prescribed."[49] This might seem like a pedantic question: for, if we were listening to an ensemble behind a curtain or else on a recording, we might never know the difference. But would that difference matter? To some people – such as Levinson – it would. Yet, if so, note that it would not be for *musical* reasons, but for *nonmusical* reasons. So it would seem that the ideal of authenticity is not wholly musical in nature. We often attach some sort of virtue to using actual period instruments *for their own sake.*

---

[49] "Authentic Performance and Performance Means," in *Music, Art, & Metaphysics* 394–5.

But we can put the argument for use of period instruments in another way. Given that musical intentions of composers are always formed in light of their historical contexts, those intentions are inevitably molded by the musical conditions of the time. For example, since Bach did not specify any particular sort of "well-tempered keyboard" for the forty-eight pieces of *Das wohltemperirte Klavier*, we could assume that he intended these to be played on a clavichord, harpsichord, organ, or (at least in the case of some of the forty-eight) an early version of the piano. These were the keyboard instruments available to Bach at the time. On this argument, it is obvious that he did not intend a modern Steinway. The problem here, however, is the status of this intention. Clearly, Bach could not have intended these pieces to be played on a Steinway. But he likewise could not have intended that they *not* be played on a Steinway. So how much can one infer from these intentions? It seems hard to get a *prohibition* from a *lack* of intention. Moreover, there is no reason to think that Bach even *thought* about such a question. And there is likewise no reason to think that he would have cared. So it is not clear here that we are still talking about the *composer's* intention.

Yet, assuming that we are attempting to duplicate something like the sound of a performance that Bach himself would have heard, the question to be asked is: *when?* At the first performance? At subsequent performances during that year? Later in life? Early music performers have sometimes attempted to answer this question by taking the *Uraufführung*, or original performance, as their standard. But there is no obvious reason to assume that the *Uraufführung* has any more claims to validity than any of the other performances Bach would have heard. Indeed, first performances often leave much to be desired and few composers would likely wish to have first performances used as the criterion against which to judge all future ones. Moreover, in most cases, composers perform their works or hear them performed

a number of times in their lifetime.[50] When we note the changes
in performance practice that have occurred in, say, the latter
half of the past century, it seems reasonable to conclude it had
not been otherwise earlier. If anything, those changes were even
more significant and swift. But there is a further complication:
not only do performing traditions change, they themselves are
never uniform. We can safely assume that there were disagreements and different points of view even within a given performance tradition of a particular era, as in our time. Rather than
being uniform and orderly, one can always find within any tradition archaic forms that are gradually falling into disuse, new
forms that are just beginning to emerge, transitional forms that
never really take root, and everything in the middle that makes
up what we consider to be the norm.

As a way of solving these problems, Davies suggests that what we
really want is "an *ideal* sound rather than as the sound of some actual, former performance."[51] But this suggestion actually proves
more problematic. Although striving for an ideal performance
frees us from being bound to imitate even poor historical performances, it ends up taking us right back to the same sorts of
difficulties facing performers attempting to be faithful to the
spirit of a composition. For, if we are looking for an ideal sound,
how are we to define this? Whereas a performance faithful to
the piece's "spirit" is difficult to specify, one attempting to reach
"an ideal sound" may be even more difficult. Whose ideal are we
talking about?

So which of these sorts of restorations truly represents a return to the essential "core" of a work of music? If we take
Harnoncourt at his word, and "accept only the composition

[50] A further complication is that it sometimes happens that a piece is never
performed in a composer's lifetime.
[51] "Authenticity in Musical Performance" 42.

itself as our source," then we are unable to conclude that Harnoncourt's performances necessarily reflect Bach's score any better than Mendelssohn's performances – except in the sense that Harnoncourt performs the whole score and Mendelssohn only a portion thereof. Harnoncourt views the romantic interpretations of the last century and earlier part of this century as attempts "to 'purify' the baroque compositions"; but is not purification likewise Harnoncourt's goal, albeit a different sort of purification? It seems difficult to say that Mendelssohn's performances truly *distorted* the pure text of Bach. Rather, it is possible to argue that Mendelssohn's revival of Bach was as much of a "return to origins" as that of Harnoncourt: why should we take the letter of a composition as being any more important than its spirit? Or perhaps we should put that a different way. Harnoncourt seems just as interested in realizing the effect that Bach intended; it is more that his idea of that effect and of how it is to be achieved are different. When Harnoncourt writes about his experience of performing the *St. Matthew Passion* for the first time and says that "every line 'spoke'" or "never before had we so intensely understood the meaning," there is no question that he is interested in far more than simply literal fidelity.[52]

Restoration faces us with an *aporia*. Literally, to be *aporos* is to be "without a way." There is no way here to decide between letter or spirit. One may compromise between them, of course (as do, I think, most if not all performances), but that still means one must *decide*. And, once we do decide (which is necessary, of course, if there is to be a performance), we face the *aporia* of *how* to be "faithful" to that letter or spirit (assuming, of course, we *decide* to

---

[52] *The Musical Dialogue* 73–4. Curiously enough, Harnoncourt also says: "What we accomplished was not the revival of an historical sound, not a museum-like restoration of sounds belonging to the past. It was a modern performance, an interpretation thoroughly grounded in the 20th century." Such a description seems exactly right.

be faithful). Restoration *always* involves making hard decisions. In cleaning and restoring paintings, for example, one must distinguish between the accumulated dirt and the work itself. Even more problematic is the fact that restoration is always two-sided: the process of "desedimenting" always entails both gain and loss. Restoring a work to its original condition often requires losing something that can be nearly as valuable as the original. A perfect illustration of this is the recent restoration of Rembrandt's painting *The Mill*. Prior to its restoration, it conveyed a somber tone by what seemed to be dark, foreboding colors – the sort of murky tones we tend to associate with Rembrandt's works. However, cleaning revealed something that we do not at all think of as typically Rembrandt: a bright sky and colorful landscape. Which one is the "real" painting? Of course, the one with bright colors is the one that is closer to what Rembrandt actually painted. Yet, we have viewed it for so long as "dark and foreboding" that there is an important sense in which – for us – it *is* dark and foreboding. Restoration reveals something that almost seems to be a different painting.[53]

But what *won't* solve this *aporia* is an appeal to "authenticity" or "integrity," since that appeal can go either way. For instance, Mark Sagoff argues in favor of a "purist" restoration, claiming that art conservators should limit their work to "cleaning works of art and to reattaching original pieces that may have fallen [off]."[54] His reason for taking this position is that, out of respect for our cultural heritage, we should preserve the integrity of art works

---

[53] We live in the midst of a continuing "reevaluation" of "Rembrandt" paintings. How many strokes *did* Rembrandt van Rijn have to put on a painting (as opposed to, say, his students and/or employees) for it to count as a "Rembrandt"? See *Rembrandt/Not Rembrandt in the Metropolitan Museum of Art: Aspects of Connoisseurship*, ed. John P. O. Neill (New York: Metropolitan Museum of Art, 1995).

[54] Mark Sagoff, "On Restoring and Reproducing Art," *Journal of Philosophy* 75 (1978) 457.

by doing as little to them as possible. But, using precisely this same argument, Yuriko Saito argues that an integral restoration is valid in some cases, since it shows our respect for the object as the artist created it.[55] As an illustration, he points out that the restoration of Leonardo da Vinci's *Last Supper*, one that not only involved cleaning but extensive repair, was necessary to restore the "integrity" of da Vinci's work, since in its pre-restoration state it was impossible to experience the work as the artist meant it to be experienced. So designating either view the "purist" view is highly misleading. Both sides are motivated by the interest in preserving the integrity of art works; the question is how one does that best.

What are we to do? Godlovitch rightly dismisses the viewpoint that musical works *should* be modernized as a viewpoint that is simply the result of our "parochial habits." There is some truth to the charge that this supposed superiority is the result of parochialism, for usually we think our performances are better largely because we are accustomed to them. Joseph Kerman makes the bold claim that "no one who has heard Beethoven's 'Moonlight' Sonata or the Sonata in D minor, Op. 31 No. 2, well played on the fortepiano will ever be entirely happy with them again on the modern piano." But would it really be impossible to be happy with them "well played" on a Steinway? To argue that hearing Beethoven on a fortepiano completely closes off all other possibilities so that one could never be satisfied with anything else is dubious at best and pretentious at worst. On the other hand, when Vaughan Williams claims that the modern piano is unquestionably superior to the harpsichord and that he has "little doubt that Bach would have thought that his music sounded better on our modern instruments than on those that

[55] Yuriko Saito, "Why Restore Works of Art?" *Journal of Aesthetics and Art Criticism* 44 (1985) 147.

he had at his disposal," he has no more support than those who argue that Bach intended his works to be played on the instruments of his day: he is simply betraying his "parochial habits," the same sort of habits that we exhibit in relation to visual art. E. H. Gombrich points out that part of the reluctance in restoring old paintings or re-painting sculpture that were once painted is that we have gotten used to them as they are now. We think of Rembrandt in terms of muted tones, which is why we are less likely to appreciate his prints: since those prints have not aged in the same way as his paintings, their colors are far brighter. But, for us, they are not "Rembrandt colors." Gombrich compares this "prejudice" with the kind of parochialism that Vaughan Williams displays: "Those who got used to the sound of the concert grand find it difficult to adjust their ears to the harpsichord."[56]

There are good reasons to eschew sloppy performances on instruments that are poor and out of tune; in short, they do not sound good to us – and, if reports from contemporaries are anything to go on, they did not sound good to listeners in other ages. *They*, however, often had to be content with far less in terms of choice. In contrast, more than perhaps any other age, we have an enormous number of opportunities and a wide variety of ways to hear excellent performers play high-quality instruments, both in live concerts and on recordings utilizing technology that comes continually closer to a live sound. In short, we can afford to be more picky. But we can also afford *not* to choose: not only is there is no reason to claim that historical performances are better than modern ones, there is no need for us to elevate one over the other. Fortunately, restorations of musical works are far

---

[56] Stan Godlovitch, "Authentic Performance," *Monist* 71 (1988) 262; Joseph Kerman, *Contemplating Music: Challenges to Musicology* (Cambridge, Mass.: Harvard University Press, 1985) 213; *National Music* 224–5; and E. H. Gombrich, *Art and Illusion: A Study of the Psychology of Pictorial Representation* (Princeton, N.J.: Princeton University Press, 1969).

less permanent than those of paintings: musical works can always be performed another way.

Of course, although they always *can* be performed in another way, there is still a kind of danger. We often grow to love them just as we have heard them. And this problem has only gotten worse – with no end in sight. In another era, it might have been the case that, having been entranced by a particular performance heard in childhood, performances heard later in life would never seem to match up. But, for us today, it is often the beloved CD – the one with a performance conducted by the famous maestro and his technically perfect orchestra (with clever editing to cover up any mistakes) without coughs or any other evidence of real human beings either making or listening to the music – that holds us in a trance and keeps us from appreciating anything *different*. Nietzsche points out that, often when we first hear a melody we find it hard to tolerate. But soon we move to the place where it so enchants us that we "become its humble and enraptured lovers who desire nothing better from the world than it and only it."[57] Recordings can have precisely that effect on us.

But, even if we could *decide* on what counts as authenticity and then actually *achieve* it musically, where would we be? While this is a different question from that of the possibility of the duplication of historical performing conditions, it is no less crucial. For, if we cannot *experience* them as the original listeners experienced them, then at least some of the "authenticity" of the performance is negated. As listeners of the early twenty-first century, our normal experience of music is such that we do not hear the sounds of Bach's *St. Matthew Passion* as the original listeners heard them and we could not hear them that way even if these original sounds could be reproduced. Moreover, we do not even hear it the way

---

[57] Friedrich Nietzsche, *The Gay Science*, trans. Walter Kaufman (New York: Random House, 1974) 262.

the audience at Mendelssohn's performance heard it. Given all of the changes in performing conditions and audience expectations that have occurred not only since Bach's own original performance but even since Mendelssohn's "original" revival of the work, our own way of experiencing the work is at least somewhat (and probably *significantly*) different from the way either of those audiences would have experienced it. And it also seems safe to say that neither of those audiences would have heard the work in exactly the same way that the other experienced it.

Yet, can we even hear what we term "modern" music in the way that the original listeners would have heard it? A good example of this is Stravinsky's *Le Sacre du Printemps*. What is now for us simply part of the concert repertoire was for the original listeners absolutely shocking and the response was so critical that it proved almost impossible to continue with the original performance. In contrast, our listening perspective is simply different from that of the riotous audience at the Théâtre des Champs-Elysées in 1913. Although *Le Sacre du Printemps* still has an arresting quality about it even today, we simply do not hear it as those listeners did. Instead, we hear it in light of even more modern music, meaning that it no longer stuns us – or at least not to the same degree.

Equally, for anyone familiar with the development of modern music, it is easy (and almost impossible not) to hear Beethoven's late string quartets as prefiguring later developments in music. Thus, we hear these quartets as *anticipating* subsequent music history, something that Beethoven's contemporaries could not have done. While they sometimes complained that his later works were inexplicably dissonant, we do not hear them that way. If anything, our problem tends to be precisely the reverse: we have heard such pieces as Beethoven's Fifth Symphony so often that many of us find it hackneyed and tiresome. Moreover, conceptions of what sounds "right" simply vary historically and culturally, which is particularly evident in terms of dissonance. What is considered dissonant in one age can be considered perfectly fine in another: for example, some jazz chords that might even border on being "kitsch" to our ears would have sounded like the worst dissonance to Mozart and his contemporaries. In the same way, we can assume that listeners in the next century will be hearing what we take to be dissonance in twentieth-century music in a very different way.

Still, *could* we hear music some other way? What Davies suggests is that dissonance, for example, is defined in terms of a style: what is dissonant in one style might not be dissonant in another. He contends that "listeners are able to make the appropriate adjustment in expectations and so come to experience music in different styles as anyone familiar with them would do, whether or not that 'anyone' is their contemporary as a listener." What he argues is that "to be *familiar* with a style will be to *experience* the dissonances within it as dissonances; that is, it will be to adjust one's expectations to match those which reflect the use of elements within the style."[58] Yet, how far can this go? We may *know* that listeners of a particular time would have experienced certain chords as dissonant; we may even try to *imagine* what their experiences might have been like; yet, that would not assure us that we could *hear* it that way. Trying to hear a chord as dissonant when it sounds perfectly normal seems akin to attempting to believe what one is convinced is false.

Precisely because early music does not sound "new" to us today means that it is alien to us. We cannot experience it as the composer's contemporaries did because it is not "our" music in the same sense that it was "theirs." However, because of the often paradoxical logic of restoration, there is a sense in which

[58] Stephen Davies, "Authenticity in Performance: A Reply to James O. Young," *British Journal of Aesthetics* 28 (1988) 374–5.

Harnoncourt's restoration likewise results in something "new" *for us.* Having become jaded by those "romantic" revivals of the *St. Matthew Passion* (not to mention *Messiah*), early music performers have served to make those tired-sounding old works live again. To us, performances from Harnoncourt or the Kuijken brothers are new and startling, maybe not in the same way as they would have been to Bach's audiences but in important ways. Thus, it makes perfect sense for Harnoncourt to say that "the familiar *St. Matthew Passion* revealed itself as an exciting new work.... We had never played it or heard it before – there was nothing with which we could associate it."[59]

Following Hegel, Gadamer argues that an essential ingredient in having a genuine experience (*Erfahrung*) is the element of surprise: it is precisely when we do not expect something that it affects us the most, which means that genuine experiences have the character of a reversal.[60] As such, they cannot be repeated again and again. This reversal is precisely what early music performances accomplish. They force us to *listen,* and it is in the act of truly listening that we have a genuine experience in which we make contact with that which we hear. But, since a genuine experience is surprising and shocking, we cannot continue to experience a piece by having it performed repeatedly in the same way. It needs to be changed, not merely so that we can hear it anew but so that we can truly hear it *at all.*

Whatever we choose, we need to be aware that it is indeed a *choice.* We can choose to "restore" music from the past by focusing on the letter or the spirit. We can also choose to perform it as we wish. But each of these options is a choice on our part. We may be able to give reasons (and perhaps even good reasons) for choosing one over the others, but we are still forced to decide.

---

[59] *The Musical Dialogue* 74–5.
[60] *Truth and Method* 353ff.

Thus, when Harnoncourt speaks of having "as few interposed optics and filters as possible" what he really wants is to have *different* optics interposed. Rather than having "forcibly repressed every sign of the present" (as Laurence Dreyfus would claim[61]), the aim of historical authenticity is *itself* a "sign of the present." It reflects twentieth-century and (now) twenty-first century musical ideals and tastes no less than Mendelssohn's performance did those of the nineteenth. Even the very goal that we have set for ourselves of being "faithful" to the composer's intentions is one peculiar to a particular era and is likewise defined in modern terms. What Hogwood says about his performances is telling: we are, he says unwittingly, interested in realizing "the Bach ideal *as we have established it.*"[62]

Clearly, our "restoration" of early music turns out to be essentially a kind of *improvisation*: for what we are doing is nothing short of improvising upon the past and using it for the present. Thus, we have no qualms about performing the *St. Matthew Passion* in a concert hall (rather than a church) or listening reverently to music that was originally designed for dancing and feasting or putting Baroque music on a compact disc (so it gets played the same way over and over again). And likely our uses are equally legitimate. Thus, not only were Bach and Beethoven in the process of making and breaking rules, so are early music performers. Of course, succeeding generations will likely be rescuing us from what they may well consider the distortion of Bach's works by early music performers of today. A paradox of restoration is that what is restored often ends up being "unrestored" by the following generations, who, though wondering how their ancestors

---

[61] Laurence Dreyfus, "Early Music Defended against its Devotees: A Theory of Historical Performance in the Twentieth Century," *Musical Quarterly* 69 (1983) 305.

[62] James Badal, "On Record: Christopher Hogwood," *Fanfare* (November-December 1985) 90 (my italics).

could have had such poor taste, find it very reassuring that they themselves at least know better.

A more troubling question, though, concerns the sedimentation itself: what is this lush growth that Harnoncourt asserts has "distorted" Bach's works? Both Husserl and Harnoncourt would seem to see it as something to be removed, as prejudices that spoil an authentic understanding or hearing. Surely prejudices can serve to obscure our hearing; but is that *all* they do? Here Harnoncourt sounds very much like Husserl, who claimed that prejudices are simply "obscurities arising out of a sedimentation of tradition."[63] There is no question that performance traditions function in essence as prejudices that color our hearing: we always (and inescapably) view and hear works of art through the grid of our tradition. However, while prejudices may obscure our vision or restrict the ways in which we are able to hear musical works, getting rid of all prejudices would be neither possible nor desirable. They provide us with a certain insight, as the "obscuring" dirt and old varnish on *The Mill* provided us with a different way of seeing an old work.

While we could argue that the early music movement tends to display a kind of Enlightenment suspicion of prejudices, there is a sense in which it is likewise a romantic movement. Gadamer points out that Romanticism can be seen as a kind of reversal of the Enlightenment, one that results in the "tendency toward restoration, i.e., the tendency to reconstruct the old because it is old."[64] But what do we actually end up with when we sweep away all the dirt? As it turns out, what early music performers really want to revive is not simply Bach's score itself. In effect, they wish to return to the way compositions were performed by composers and their contemporaries. Rather than finding the pure Bach,

---

[63] *The Crisis of European Sciences* 72.
[64] *Truth and Method* 273.

we end up with an interpretation contemporaneous with him – if we turn out to be lucky (and, of course, we would never know). In one sense, this concern could be characterized as a deeper respect for the past. Yet, this respect turns out again to be highly selective. The privileging of the original past means *a privileging of one past over another.* Thus, while there is an interest in the past, there is no interest in the *intervening* past. Or, perhaps we could say that, while we have a respect for the past, we have considerably less respect for the tradition that has preserved it for us. In effect, there is a denial of the richness of everything in between: all that counts is that *early* tradition. So there is no appreciation for the gift that has been bequeathed to us by the *entire* history. What Gadamer terms the *Wirkungsgeschichte* – the effects that art works have had over the years – is seen as having little value.

Certainly, to deny the historical context in which musical compositions of the past arose would be to deny a key element: as Harnoncourt recognizes, Bach's *St. Matthew Passion* is not simply timeless but also time-linked. But *another* aspect of the time-linked character of the *St. Matthew Passion* is its history through the centuries: what it has become to us over the years. Note that there is no reason to think that Bach's contemporaries thought the piece to be anything special. Instead, it was just one of the hundreds of compositions that Bach composed for the choir in Leipzig. Only to *us* has it become important. Its history, then, would seem to be at least as important (if not more important) than any performances of Bach's day. Like Kierkegaard's disciple at second hand – whom Kierkegaard thought was actually more privileged in some ways than the original ones – we are in the position of being able to look back and see the developing of that history and what it has meant to our predecessors.[65]

---

[65] See Søren Kierkegaard, *Philosophical Fragments*, trans. David Swenson and Howard Hong (Princeton, N.J.: Princeton University Press, 1962).

There is no reason for us to want to go back, even if it were possible. But there is something else that we must not forget: our modern perspective of Bach owes much more to Mendelssohn's performance than we care to admit. It was Mendelssohn and his contemporaries (certainly not Bach's contemporaries) that first came to value the *St. Matthew Passion* as a great work. In considering Bach's works to be among the greatest of our cultural heritage, we stand firmly in the tradition of Mendelssohn and his contemporaries.

But there is something far more troubling than this lack of appreciation for the past. For the past is not merely a collection of performances that are themselves gifts to us (even *if* we decide that, as gifts, they likewise distorted what they were supposed to be passing along). Those performances – and the performance tradition – were only possible because of *performers*. Thus, our lack of gratitude is a lack of gratitude to specific human beings who, at least in many cases, were probably trying their best. And so there is a deep *ethical* component to this lack of appreciation. Strangely enough, though early music performers have often justified their performances precisely on the basis of being "true" to the composer and so considered themselves to be "ethically responsible," that ingratitude to the intervening past in effect has made them ethically *irresponsible*. We shall return to this question of respecting the past in Chapter 5. But certainly there is no easy answer to how one "best" respects the past or does it justice.

In any case, our performances of early music bear our own distinct stamp and this reveals much about the essential structure of restoration. While we tend to think of restoration as a kind of "resurrection" of the past, that resurrection is never one in which the original aural structure is simply raised from the dead: instead, it takes on a new body. Restoration cannot help but situate the past in a new context, since the reactivation of the past requires bringing it into the present, not somehow turning the present into the past. That means, of course, that the handing down of tradition is never completely smooth; rather, restoration, by its very nature, involves *both* continuity *and* discontinuity, *both* gain *and* loss. So we are always "reinventing" the past. As the pianist Edward Steuermann notes:

> Contrary to general belief, there are no fixed rules . . . you must always, in accordance with your musical vision, solve once more, as if they had been invented yesterday, even the simplest problems, thus making the music new and alive, and saving it from petrification. Here, I believe, is the instance where musical notation can give only a hint; here the interpreter is confronted with the task which calls for all his really creative forces.[66]

Not only are performers always involved in improvising (however limited or unlimited that may be) on the music that they play but also they are – right along with the composer – making and breaking the rules that form the tradition of which they are both a part.

But, if *both* composition and performance result in the modification of the discourse in which they takes place, then there is no escaping the conclusion that a musical work's identity is also in flux, for we have seen that it is clearly tied to the context in which it exists. Of course, we must be careful not to overemphasize this point: for, while a work's identity is indeed determined in a significant way by its context, that identity is still reasonably stable (an issue to which we shall return in Chapter 4). Moreover, that the work exists *amidst* this improvisational process means that the performer is truly a part of the composition of that work – not merely an appendage. As Vaughan Williams puts it, "a musical

[66] Edward Steuermann, *The Not Quite Innocent Bystander: Writings of Edward Steuermann*, ed. Clara Steuermann, David Porter, and Gunther Schuller, trans. Richard Cantwell and Charles Messner (Lincoln: University of Nebraska Press, 1989) 102n1.

composition when invented is only half finished, and until actual sound is produced that composition *does not exist*."[67]

So composition is by nature a *multipart invention*, one that begins before the composer and continues far after the composer is finished. How might we *rethink* such a reality?

[67] *National Music* 123 (Vaughan Williams's italics).

FOUR

The *Ergon* within *Energeia*

Regarded in its true nature, *language* is an enduring thing, and at every moment a *transitory* one. Even its maintenance by writing is always just an incomplete, mummy-like preservation, only needed again in attempting to picture the living utterance. In itself it is no product (*Ergon*), but an activity (*Energeia*). Its true definition therefore can only be a genetic one.[1]

So WHAT RESULTS FROM THE IMPROVISATORY MOVEMENT OF composition and performance? From musical *energeia* grows an *ergon* – but an *ergon* that still remains *within* the play of musical *energeia*, and from which it cannot be disconnected. Indeed, we might more properly say that this *ergon* exists as *energeia*. Thus, improvisation provides a way of conceptualizing music that does not force us to choose between defining music as either *ergon* or *energeia*. Music that is improvised endures and is yet transitory. Being transitory, its existence is very much genetic, historical, changing; but, in that it likewise endures, it has a continuing identity.

[1] Wilhelm von Humboldt, *On Language: The Diversity of Human Language-Structure and Its Influence on the Mental Development of Mankind*, trans. Peter Heath (Cambridge: Cambridge University Press, 1988) 49 (von Humboldt's italics, translation modifed).

To see music as essentially improvisational clearly has certain implications for musical activity. First, while we need not necessarily see the creation of musical works as incompatible with the activity of music making – indeed, they can be seen as interdependent – the *telos* of music making cannot be defined simply in terms of the creation of musical works, or even primarily so. Instead, the work becomes a *means* to the end of making music, not an end in itself. Second, if the work exists within the play of musical *energeia*, then it cannot be seen as autonomous or detached. Like a living organism, it is ever in motion and constantly in need of care and infusions of new life to keep it alive. Third, if performers are essentially improvisers, then authorship becomes more complex. That is not to deny composers their respective place as "authors" or to take away the respect that they truly deserve; but it *is* to acknowledge that their authorship is really a *co*authorship, both with those who have gone before and those who come after. What comes into being in musical *energeia* is something that composer, performer, and listener all have a hand in creating.

How might we explain this elusive thing that exists within musical *energeia*? Surprisingly enough, Ingarden's account provides important clues.

The Elusive "Work Itself"

Central to Ingarden's phenomenology of music is the assumption that there is not merely an accidental but an essential separation between the work and its written and aural embodiments. Ingarden wants to defend at any cost the *ergon* that remains beyond the reach of the effects of musical *energeia*. But what is remarkable about Ingarden is that he is so unwilling simply to ignore the tensions that threaten the very autonomy of the work he doggedly wishes to defend that his account ends up being in tension with itself. Precisely this is what makes it highly instructive. Ingarden is well aware that the real question of the work's identity is not merely static ontologically but also (and essentially) historical in nature. As he puts it: "The 'old' works 'live' – that means, to begin with, that they are played and heard – in successively new musical epochs and are constantly performed somewhat differently in various respects in each new epoch."[2] But what is *it* that lives on?

To begin, in what sense are the work and the score related? We noted earlier that Ingarden sees the score as having the crucial function of preserving the work. Thus he assures us that, as long as the score exists, "there cannot, therefore, be any doubt about the musical work's identity in the course of history": for "the score clearly determines the limits" of the work. It would seem, then, that the work has a reasonably well-delimited identity, as long as the score exists. Yet, we also have seen that Ingarden recognizes that the score is at best a kind of schema, one that is only capable of preserving certain aspects of the work, since he claims that "this schematic formation does not exhaust the musical work." But this leaves us with a kind of dilemma. On the one hand, if the score is what assures the identity of the work, it would seem that the work ends up being practically – even if not theoretically – no more (and no less) than the score. Anything *more* would be a surplus that goes beyond the strict identity of the work. On the other hand, Ingarden clearly suggests that the work is in some sense both *other* than and *more* than the score. Not only does this throw the identity of the work into jeopardy, it also raises the key ontological question of what constitutes this *more*. Is there something that guarantees the identity of this surplus that goes beyond the score? Moreover, what connection is there – if any – between this more and musical *energeia*?[3]

---

[2] *Ontology of the Work of Art* 104.
[3] Ibid. 106, 113, and 120.

The elusiveness of the work is perhaps even better illuminated by the role of performances. What exactly accounts for differences between performances? Ingarden's view is that the work has "a constant stock of possibilities belonging to it." So there is a sense in which the work is inherently complete. Thus, "the historical process of the alleged transformation of the musical work itself is in reality only a process of discovering and actualizing ever new possibilities of the potential forms of the work belonging to the work schema." Those possibilities are not really added by performers but rather discovered. As a result, the work only *appears* to change. But the problem with this view is that – practically – these possibilities seem not to come merely from *within* but also from *without*: for they arise – at least partly – by way of performance traditions, which are themselves developing. As it turns out, Ingarden himself implies that the work is somehow in progress. He says that "the actual work . . . grows beyond the artistic intent of the composer" (due to its places of indeterminacy). So Ingarden wants to say that – somehow – musical works are *live* and even *growing* entities.[4]

There are at least three ways of characterizing this "growth." First, we may be able to harmonize these two ideas of Ingarden (that is, that works have a "stock of possibilities" and that they grow "beyond the artistic intent of the composer") by saying that, while musical works have a kind of set identity at the point of composition, the composer may not always be (or, more likely, never is) aware of all possibilities. On this account, works don't actually "change"; rather, their various facets just come to light over time. Thus, musical works are – from their *Ursprung* – relatively "thick" in nature. Second, we might instead claim that musical works are merely "schemas" that are "filled in" over time by way of external influences (such as performing traditions and uses

---

[4] Ibid. 114 and 120.

to which they are put). According to this account, works are only minimally constituted by scores (and perhaps a little more, such as the constraints of the performance tradition at the time of composition). All of the things that are added in performances, then, merely "fill out" the bare outline. Here we have a comparatively "thin" conception of works, in which works themselves (and not merely our perception of them) "develop." Third, we might combine these two views, with the result that works *do* have a "stock of possibilities" that constitute them, but those possibilities are in turn supplemented by further possibilities that arise over the life of the work. On this view, a composer may indeed have a complex conception of the work (and so potentially a relatively complex set of "intentions"), but those intentions are supplemented by actual performances and the development of performance traditions. Thus, we could say that Bach had intentions for the *St. Matthew Passion* that were complex and specific. But the performance by Mendelssohn did not *merely* bring out those possibilities (even though it did that *too*). Rather, it also *created* certain possibilities – possibilities that truly did not exist before.

To choose the first view is, in effect, to choose a Platonist view. For, if the work contains a set of possibilities that are unknown to the composer but are actually *inherent in the work*, then we can only properly characterize "composing" as discovery of what already exists. Performing *too* could be characterized as "discovery," so that both Mendelssohn's and Harnoncourt's performances are discoveries of inherent possibilities. Of course, one could still speak of the composer as "creating" a work (as does Wolterstorff) in the sense that it becomes a part of our cultural existence. But it is hard to see how the question of "discovery" versus "creation" can be resolved without appeal to circular argument. Either the view in which works already possess their full range of possibilities is intuitively compelling or it is not. In my case, I find it hard to believe that all possibilities – including ones not only not envisioned by the composer but also ones that the composer *could not have envisioned* – have always been inherent in the work from the moment of its *Ursprung* or even the *Fassung letzter hand*. And these complications grow exponentially in the practice of jazz or blues. But, of course, any Platonist could simply argue – in return – that these complications are merely apparent ones: for the problem is just that we do not *know* what possibilities were there all along. So what seems to be an *ontological* problem is more an *epistemological* problem.

In any case, even if we say that works never *really* grow beyond their original boundaries, they certainly *appear* to do so. In other words, our *conception* of a given work truly does change over time. And, since in the first view no one (neither performer nor even composer) has access to all of the possibilities of a given work, the distinction turns out to be one that cannot be proved or disproved. Moreover, it has little significance in musical practice. For one could always argue that *any* given improvisational possibility belongs *essentially* to a work (however seemingly inappropriate). Given a lack of access to the true essence of a work, there would be no way to adjudicate the claim. One could, of course, respond that such an interpretation seemed "implausible." But that response would be just as available to someone who held the second position. So, *practically*, there is no difference.

If we return to Ingarden, we see that he is left in a curious position. For, if musical works have the virtue of being unchanging because of somehow transcending the vicissitudes of musical *energeia*, then this very removal clearly means that no one ever really experiences a musical work. Indeed, Ingarden admits precisely this: "Strictly speaking, we never become acquainted with a given musical work as the ideal aesthetic object." On Ingarden's account, then, the work itself turns out to be something that *no one ever hears.*[5]

But there is a much deeper problem in Ingarden's account – a basic contradiction that is never really resolved. On the one hand, Ingarden reassures us that the problem of the work's identity is an *illusory* one that only arises if we confuse its various profiles with the work itself. Once we properly understand its ideal character and realize that the work itself is a "superhistorical formation," then "the problem of the identity of the work disappears." For, being an entity that stands outside of history, its identity is assured. What, though, is this ahistorical formation? Ingarden tells us that it is *not* "a concrete object that in the course of historical time itself undergoes various changes as a consequence of changes of concrete historical conditions." Rather, "the work itself, which is determined by the score in some of its components and features, transcends the score and differs more or less from each performance." Thus, the work must be at least in some sense autonomous from either score or performance. On the other hand, Ingarden likewise thinks that musical works have an *Ursprung* and are thus historical in origin. In this respect, his view of ideal objects is similar to Husserl's view. Moreover, he claims that musical works are "with respect to their properties, in the last analysis dependent on the gradually forming intersubjective conception of the work."[6] So, even though the work is something that we never hear, the properties of the work are constituted *intersubjectively* – and over time.

Ingarden is left somewhere *between* these two possibilities – wanting to retain the "superhistorical" character of the work (to keep it "untouched" by time) but acknowledging its birth in time

[5] Ibid. 108.
[6] Ibid. 110, 115, and 119–20.

and dependence upon our "conception" of the work. But, once Ingarden connects the work with the real world, then he is forced to choose. For the work can no longer be "superhistorical." Thus, it would seem that the work is "in the last analysis" (to use Ingarden's phrase) in some way dependent on the various ways in which not merely the composer but also the performers and listeners apprehend the work. Yet, if the work is historical (within history) rather than superhistorical (outside of history), then it is impossible for Ingarden to keep the *ergon* distinct from the musical *energeia*. Although not in so many words, Ingarden in effect acknowledges the dependence of the *ergon* on musical *energeia* by his notion of *Unbestimmtheitsstellen*. As a result, the history of musical works simply *is* a history of shifting perceptions. Precisely because Ingarden is such a careful phenomenologist, he shows us that it is impossible to maintain that either a work's existence or its identity is utterly disconnected from its aural embodiments.

But, given this interconnectedness of work and performance, perhaps we should simply stop thinking in terms of "works." For the notion of a work implies something autonomous, something disconnected from musical *energeia*. What term might we use? I suggest that we go back to a much older term, that of "piece."[7] In contrast to the notion of the work, the idea of a *piece* implies something that is connected to a contextual whole – and apart from which it cannot exist. The OED defines a "piece" as a "part, bit, or fragment."[8] Furthermore, whereas a work suggests something complete in itself at the moment of its completion, a piece would seem to be inherently *incomplete*, for the musical context

---

[7] The English term "piece" was applied to music at least as early as 1601, when Shakespeare has a character in *Twelfth Night* ask for "that peece [*sic*] of song." In French, one finds *la pièce de musique* and *le morceau detaché*. The German equivalent is *das musikalische Stück*.

[8] *The Oxford English Dictionary*, 2nd ed., s.v. "piece."

in which it exists is in flux. So what sort of *living* existence does a piece of music have? How does this *ergon* inhabit musical *energeia*?

To answer that question, we need to consider (1) the degree of spontaneity of improvisation, as well as the parallel between "composition" and "improvisation," (2) the difference (and similarity) between improvisation and performance, and (3) the way in which a piece of music provides a kind of "space" for dwelling musically and how that dwelling alters the piece itself.

Premeditated Spontaneity

We have seen that our usual way of thinking about performance is that it is a kind of material instantiation of an ideal entity, making performance *more* (even if not completely) a matter of representation than of presentation. In contrast, improvisation would seem to be a *presentation* of something that is created at that moment. Thus, whereas performance might be characterized in terms of premeditated repetition, improvisation appears to be a sort of spontaneous presentation. But just how much of a difference is there between performance and improvisation?

In Chapter 2, we saw that our conception of musical composition has been defined largely in terms of the Kantian notion of the genius as "creator" who is engaged in making and breaking the rules. But we also noted that the actual reality of composition is somewhat different from what this mythical picture would have us believe. Rather, I argued that composers are more accurately described as *improvisers,* for composition essentially involves a kind of improvisation on the already existing rules and limits in such a way that what emerges is the result of both respecting those rules and altering them.

So is improvisation more like performance or composition? According to the usual conception of improvisation, it is most like the latter. Like the demiurge composer, we tend to think of the improvising musician as being out there "all alone," unconstrained by any rules. Indeed, the image is that of the improviser as the ultimate musical risk taker, and jazz musicians (for instance) have tended to play up that image. So both composers and improvisers are often seen as true "creators." But improvisers – at least in one sense – have the edge over composers in that their "creation" is done publicly, without the chance for correction. When an improviser makes a mistake there is no "net" – no score that spells things out – to rely on and no "eraser" (at least in live performance). This uncertainty is one of the most exhilarating aspects of improvised music. As Hegel noted in speaking of the improvising performer, "we have present before us not merely a work of art but the actual production of one."[9] Moreover, this "work" may come into being with certain frailties left intact – notes that might not sound quite "right," runs or progressions that get away even from the performer, and the uncertainty of knowing where all of this is going. Lee B. Brown (rightly) points out that these so-called imperfections are part of why (at least some of us) celebrate jazz.[10]

Yet, how spontaneous really is jazz improvisation? Or, to put this question differently, when the artist/jazz musician Sam Rivers says "there's nothing I can do wrong [sic], nothing," to what extent can we take this seriously?[11] The answer, of course, depends on the sorts of constraints – that is, standards and expectations – a given practice imposes on its practioners. The

---

[9] *Aesthetics: Lectures on Fine Art* 956.
[10] Lee B. Brown, "'Feeling My Way': Jazz Improvisation and Its Vicissitudes – A Plea for Imperfection," *Journal of Aesthetics and Art Criticism* 58 (2000) 113–23. Also see Ted Gioria, *The Imperfect Art: Reflections on Jazz and Modern Culture* (New York: Oxford University Press, 1988).
[11] "Modern Jazz Pioneer Sam Rivers Profiled," National Public Radio, Weekend Edition, 03-28-1998.

jazz composer and musician Carla Bley describes her compositions as follows: "I write pieces that are like drawings in a crayon book and the musicians color them themselves."[12] From what we have seen, not just Bley's pieces but all pieces are essentially like coloring book pictures. But obviously the *coloring* that occurs in different musical practices is hardly the same. How much one needs (or is allowed) to color them in depends on the limitations provided by a particular musical practice and individual pieces. Yet, coloring never stays purely within the lines. For the "coloring in" that takes place in performance also consists of redefining those lines or, alternatively, redefining what it means to respect them.

Now, if we take the example of what is called "free jazz" (of which Rivers is a practitioner) there are relatively few "materials" and "norms." So, perhaps Rivers is correct – with a little allowance for hyperbole. But clearly *most* jazz musicians operate by way of some sorts of constraints, some sort of framework – however loose, however subject to change, however unspoken – that provides the lines for jazz coloring. In some forms of jazz (such as that originating in New Orleans), that framework is comparatively rigid. But, even in more "open" sorts of jazz that framework is not lacking: it may be a typical thirty-two bar form, a standard blues form, a collection of musical motifs, or simply a sketchy verbal agreement ahead of time. One of the best-known jazz albums, *Kind of Blue*, is said to be primarily the product of sketches brought into the studio by Miles Davis about a half hour before recording.[13] And this limited framework is undoubtedly further reduced in what is called "free jazz." Yet, while it might appear to be the very absence of any framework, "free" jazz is

---

[12] This quotation comes directly from Ms. Bley herself.

[13] See the liner notes [Sony B000002ADT] by Bill Evans, pianist on this recording. Of course, one might question whether there was any "romanticizing" by Evans on the details.

not quite without "lines." Sam Rivers or Ornette Coleman may push the boundaries of jazz in many ways. But clearly they are not just playing "anything." The limitations on "free" improvisation are even more evident in such cases as when, on her "Piano Jazz" radio program, Marian McPartland attempts something like free improvisation. While she is clearly not following a set tune, her "free" improvisations tend to have a similar sort of form and utilize many of the same chords (which tend to follow a pattern of being more dissonant than her usual chord changes).

Improvisation (whether in jazz or in Eastern genres) is far more organized than it might appear.[14] Many of these limitations come from the tradition in which they have arisen, in the sense that improvising is based on and can only be understood in light of the entire tradition of improvising that has gone on before. Not merely at an early stage but even throughout a musician's career what is improvised bears the marks of other improvisers, not infrequently in the form of quotation. It is impossible to escape the influence of the past in the improvisations of the present. For improvisation is a kind of "composition" in the sense of "putting together." One takes the basic rhythmic and chord structures of the genre in which one works and puts them together in different ways. In the same way that Rudolf Bernet points out that "somebody who must hold a lecture discovers that he or she is continually paraphrasing other authors and speaks as well in the name of colleagues and friends," so jazz musicians realize from the very beginning how much they speak in the name of others and thus how much they owe to them.[15] As would be expected, of course, jazz musicians develop their

[14] See Bruno Nettl, "Thoughts on Improvisation: A Comparative Approach," *Musical Quarterly* 60 (1974) 1–19.

[15] Rudolf Bernet, "The Other in Myself," in *Deconstructive Subjectivities*, ed. Simon Critchley and Peter Dews (Albany: State University of New York Press, 1996) 177.

own repertoire of phrases and ways of saying something, so that (just as in ordinary speech) one often quotes oneself (and in the process also quotes others).[16] But those phrases and ways of speaking are never fully their "own." Indeed, it is the recognition that jazz is not *merely* spontaneous that prompted some of Adorno's harshest criticism of jazz: for his charge is that "what appears as spontaneity is in fact carefully planned out in advance."[17] His critique is perhaps best summarized by the title of his essay – "Perennial Fashion: Jazz." On Adorno's view, jazz is characterized by a perennial sameness defined by its stock of threadbare clichés.

Here it is helpful to ask: what makes improvisation *possible?* Like composition and performance, improvisation is also a practice requiring *technē*, a kind of practical knowledge (or skill) that can be learned.[18] It, too, "involves standards of excellence and obedience to rules as well as the achievement of goods." If I wish to become part of that practice, I must "accept the authority of those standards and the inadequacy of my own performance as judged by them."[19] The first thing an aspiring jazz musician must do is recognize her present inability, which may be painful and perhaps even slightly humiliating. It is remarkably humbling to hear one's teacher play, say, your saxophone – and then try it

[16] Note that even the highly inventive improvisations of Charlie Parker were actually composed out of about one hundred basic musical ideas, runs, and phrases. See Charles O. Hartman, *Jazz Text: Voice and Improvisation in Poetry, Jazz, and Song* (Princeton, N.J.: Princeton University Press, 1991) 78.

[17] Theodor W. Adorno, "Perennial Fashion – Jazz," in *Prisms*, trans. Samuel and Shierry Weber (Cambridge, Mass.: MIT Press, 1981) 123. Of course, Adorno here is commenting on *early* jazz that (at least generally) *was* less "spontaneous" than more recent jazz.

[18] See *Nicomachean Ethics* VI, 3–4 in *The Complete Works of Aristotle*, Vol. II, ed. Jonathan Barnes (Princeton, N.J.: Princeton University Press, 1984) 1139b14–1140a23.

[19] *After Virtue* 190.

oneself; so humbling that one is tempted to think that – somewhere between those two actions – an ontological change to the instrument must have occurred.

Of course, "standards of excellence" and what counts as "obedience to rules" differs not merely from practice to practice but also *over time*.[20] Earlier, I noted that classic New Orleans jazz is – in comparison to later forms of jazz – relatively "simple." The chords are not particularly complex, one improvises within relatively strict boundaries, and solos are restricted (which means, practically, that one has far less of the sense of being "out there all by oneself"). But other forms of jazz push those chords (sometimes a great deal), have greater room for and even strong expectations of far more complex improvisation, and place a great deal of emphasis on solos (so that perhaps the other members of the group even step off the stage for a break during a solo). So there are evolving standards of excellence and definitions of obedience to rules. And those changes may even lead to the development of "subpractices" within practices (so that New Orleans jazz can be considered a "subpractice" within jazz itself).

Here, Kant's notion of the genius is instructive, for the genius is (at least according to Kant) the one who opens up new ways of thinking and seeing. Translated into either jazz or classical music, the genius is the one who offers us new ways of hearing and playing. Not just new chordal and rhythmic ways of being but new ways of even conceiving what good playing sounds like. So, while there are certainly "standards" and the requirement of something like "obedience," those standards and what counts as obedience to them are subject to change. Jazz, of course, is certainly not alone in this respect. Even Classical music of the

---

[20] One example of a change in the ideal of "performing well" in classical music is the shift from the emphasis on "expression" in the romantic performance tradition to the more "literal" interpretations of "historically attuned" performers.

narrow sort (Haydn to Beethoven) evidences significant changes along the way in both standards of excellence and obedience conditions (as we have already chronicled). And, despite the fact that we live in an age in which "classical music" (broadly defined) is relatively "backward looking" and "fundamentalistic" in performance practice, there are still signs of change.[21]

To be a musician – whether classified as a "composer" or "performer" – is not only to know certain things but to have so internalized these skills that one *acts* as a musician acts.[22] And, whether one is improvising in the jazz tradition or simply trying for some sort of *Werktreue*, the goal is never simply imitation. But one doesn't reach that stage for quite some time. A great deal of learning is mimetic. One does not simply build "something" but inevitably follows the patterns that already exist. Like any practice or craft, playing music is an ability that one gains through a combination of learning essential elements and understanding how they are to be utilized. One often (though certainly not always) begins with musical basics: scales, modes, arpeggios, and chords. Once the beginner has a basic "feel" for such elements, it is possible to begin putting them together. Of course, while there may be better or worse ways to plunge into the world of jazz or classical music or blues or rock, there is no particular order in which one must begin. One could, for example, learn all

---

[21] Consider, for example, how the limits of what can be performed in a concert hall have significantly expanded in the past decade alone. And that is not simply a matter of, say, allowing jazz musicians to perform in a concert hall. The *very practice* of classical musicians has opened up so that performers like the Kronos Quartet can play arrangements of music by Jimi Hendrix without simply being classified as "rock musicians."

[22] Part of becoming a musician requires establishing a *musical* connection of mind and body. Following Merleau-Ponty, we could say that a bodily intentionality of a particular sort develops. See Elizabeth A. Behnke, "At the Service of the Sonata: Music Lessons with Merleau-Ponty," in *Merleau-Ponty: Critical Essays*, ed. Henry Pietersma (Washington, D.C.: University Press of America, 1989) 23–9.

of the scales, modes, arpeggios, and chords theoretically *before* one ever plays a note. Or one could start with three chords and learn to improvise on them, not even knowing that there were such things as scales or chords.[23] Most jazz musicians probably start somewhere in between.[24] Or, as is often the case in classical music instruction, one begins with simple pieces complemented by exercises. But, however one begins, in the same way that children first speak largely on the basis of imitating their parents, so beginning students learn by imitation. Jazz musicians often learn to play whole solos of past masters such as Charlie Parker or Art Tatum (or more current figures).[25]

While one never creates "out of nothing," flat imitation falls considerably short of what we expect of improvisers – and even of "faithful" performers of classical music. How, then, does one

[23] In my only brush with jazz "instruction," that was exactly how the first session began. We were simply given the three basic chords of the key of D (dorian mode – all "white" notes), the easiest key in which to begin. And the instructor then said: "Ok, play." Since *I* had already studied the technical elements of music, I know what we were doing. But the other students had very little clue. Interestingly enough, it proved to be a highly successful technique.

[24] Note that there is a kind of unavoidable (though not necessarily *undesirable*) sort of circularity about "joining" a practice. How does one *become* a jazz musician or a musician of any kind? The answer is: by *being* one. In order to swim, one has to jump into the water. At what point, then, is one *swimming* (as opposed to merely, say, floundering)? There isn't any obvious line of demarcation here of when one counts as a "musician." Is it when your parents actually *enjoy* listening to you practice? Or when you take part in a recital? Or when someone actually pays you to play (instead of not to play)?

[25] Although one can learn to be a jazz improviser by studying with a teacher (the way in which most classical musicians begin), the history of jazz improvisation would lead us to the conclusion that patterns for improvisation have often been picked up much less formally. There are various implications to this less formal sort of initiation into the *technē* of jazz, but certainly one of them is that jazz musicians have tended to have a more practical than theoretical knowledge.

go beyond? One of the things we most expect of improvisers is spontaneity, the ability to make split-second choices in the heat of the moment. Not unlike a composer, the improviser's task is that of making choices – choosing to play one thing instead of another, taking one path in place of all of the others that beckon. Such an ability seems not only difficult to define but also not the sort of thing one could "learn." Indeed, if we assume that a *technē* requires reliable rules of governance that can be taught, then it would seem that jazz, for instance, could not qualify as a *technē*. For what would it mean to "teach" the "rules" of spontaneity? Of course, historically there are many accounts of *technē*, some of which considerably downplay the reliability of rules (making them at best something like "rules of thumb") and the possibility of teaching (making it at best a kind of cultivation of "sensitivity").[26] If jazz improvisation can possibly count as a *technē*, then it must surely be on the more "open" rather than "closed" end of the spectrum, since the "teaching" of improvisation clearly amounts to something like "learn what I do in order to go beyond what I do." Of course, one can argue that *good* teaching simply has that sort of structure.

While the very idea of a "planned improvisation" sounds almost like an oxymoron, there is no reason to think that being spontaneous is incompatible with thinking about what one will play or even practicing ahead of time. Clearly, the question of spontaneity is more one of degree – how *much* a particular improvisation is planned in advance and how much actually happens "in the moment" – than a purely qualitative difference. Although Brown rightly notes that "improvisers do not create *ex nihilo*," his account (at least on my read) *overemphasizes* the degree to which

---

[26] See David Roochnik's *Of Art and Wisdom: Plato's Understanding of Techne* (University Park: Pennsylvania State University Press, 1996). He contrasts a rigid with a more flexible sense of the term (pp. 21–2 and 52–3).

an improviser is "creating [the music] as she plays."[27] Assuredly, *some* of what happens in a particular improvisation – no matter how planned – *is* decided in the split second of the moment. Thus, improvisation inevitably involves "a constantly changing balance between material planned in advance and spontaneous extemporisation."[28] And, if music can be seen as a kind of conversation, this should hardly be surprising. As long as one is playing with others, simply the interaction among the players means that whatever any one player has decided in advance (or even what they have all decided in advance) is always left uncertain. To the extent that the dialogue is a genuine dialogue, it is impossible to know exactly what is going to happen before it takes place. But, even if one is simply playing *alone*, there is still a degree of spontaneity. For improvisations still have a way of developing on their own, so that one is never completely in control and can never be certain in advance about what will happen. And even playing in a string quartet has some degree of this "spontaneity."

However, despite the fact that improvisations can develop in ways that astound even those playing them, jazz musicians (for example) have themselves often recognized that improvisation – or at least what they consider good improvisation – is never merely spontaneous. Duke Ellington observes: "There has never been anybody who has blown even two bars worth listening to who didn't have some idea about what he was going to play, before he started."[29] As odd as it may sound, the musician who is most prepared – not only in terms of having thought about what is

[27] Lee B. Brown, "Musical Works, Improvisation, and the Principle of Continuity," *Journal of Aesthetics and Art Criticism* 54 (1996) 354.
[28] Alan Durant, "Improvisation in the Political Economy of Music," in *Music and the Politics of Culture*, ed. Christopher Norris (New York: St. Martin's Press, 1989) 267.
[29] Ken Rattenbury, *Duke Ellington: Jazz Composer* (New Haven, Conn.: Yale University Press, 1990) 14.

to be played but even having played various possibilities – is most able to be spontaneous. It is when one already is prepared that one feels free to go beyond the confines of the prepared (with the assurance that one can always fall back on them if necessary). In the same way that Gadamer argues that the experienced person is most open to new experience, it is the experienced improviser – the one who has already thought a great deal about what is to be played – who is most able to play something surprising. Experience can turn into a rut, but it can also beget spontaneity.

Perhaps the key to the question of spontaneity – indeed to the very distinction between performance and improvisation – is the role of interpretation. Philip Alperson suggests that

> interpretation, a prime feature of conventional musical performance, may be safely said to be absent from an improvisation: it makes no sense to characterize an improvisation as an interpretation or to praise it as a good interpretation of a previously existing work since no such work exists.[30]

Yet, *pace* Alperson, I think improvisation is *fundamentally* interpretive in nature. What is crucial here is the underlying definition of interpretation being assumed, for this definition is at the heart of the distinction between performance and improvisation. Note that interpretation (like performance) is taken here to be essentially repetitive in nature. Thus, whereas a performance can be seen as an interpretation because it appears to *re*present an already existing "work," an improvisation does not seem to represent anything having a prior existence. Instead, so the assumption goes, the "work" comes into being *in the very act of performance* (or such is the assumption that Alperson makes).

---

[30] Philip Alperson, "On Musical Improvisation," *Journal of Aesthetics and Art Criticism* 63 (1984) 26.

Yet, this (questionable) assumption in no way means that improvisation does not involve interpretation.

While the interpretation required in the performance of a piece of classical music *is* a kind of repetition, it is (as we have already seen) always far more than that. The reason is that the mimetic movement of interpretation is likewise the introduction of a supplement. And this is the case (in varying degrees, of course) whether we are talking about performing classical music, jazz, Indian raga, blues, and probably most types of music. To take jazz as our example, the most obvious sense in which a jazz improvisation is interpretive is that the vast majority of jazz consists of improvisations *on* particular tunes. The pianist Tommy Flanagan says that "soloists elaborate upon what the structure of the piece has to say."[31] Of course, an improvisation may end up moving very far from the tune – and, to the untrained ear, the interpretations of the most creative musicians may at times seem to have little to do with the original "text" (especially in those cases where the melody is never played and the harmonic structure has changed radically). But the presence of the tune's original structure will usually still be felt (and one evidence of this is that jazz musicians, for instance, often hum the tune – sometimes even audibly – while improvising on it). Even in the case of, say, Bill Evans's various improvisations on "All of You," which seem (at least to the untrained ear) to have almost nothing to do with the tune listed on the liner notes, it is clear to someone truly familiar with the piece that it is still a kind of interpretation of it, albeit an interpretation that simply cannot be explained very well by a merely repetitive conception of interpretation.

One way of accounting for the difference between the kind of interpretation typical of classical music performers and jazz musicians is that the latter simply have far more room for creative

[31] *Thinking in Jazz* 170.

interpretation. Yet, many jazz musicians would assuredly argue for the validity of their improvising on precisely the same basis used by such earlier classical music performers as Mendelssohn and Landowska: that of capturing the spirit of the tune precisely by ignoring the letter. It is sometimes uncanny how an improvisation can capture the mood of a piece better than a simple repetition of it.

But there is a much wider sense in which jazz can be seen as interpretive. Not only do most jazz improvisations center around a particular tune, they are likewise – in an equally important sense – interpretations of the entire tradition. Of course, this is also the case in classical music, since a performance is always based on both the score and the whole performance tradition that surrounds it. If I play a piece of Chopin, it is almost impossible for me not to have been influenced by the entire Chopin performance tradition (a large tradition indeed), particularly as embodied by such recent performers as Brendel or Vladimir Horowitz or Sviatoslav Richter. There is a very real sense in which I interpret not just the score but also *their* interpretations. And they, in turn, represent "interpretations" of others in that tradition. Given the wider limits of interpretation allowed in jazz, this sense of indebtedness to performers of the past (and present) tends to be even stronger. If I am playing "April in Paris," I have the very real sense that I am not merely playing a tune by Vernon Duke but a tune that has been interpreted by Count Basie, Charlie Parker, and Joe Pass. It is a Vernon Duke tune, but it is likewise a Basie tune. I interpret the tune, but my interpretation is likewise an interpretation of those previous interpretations. And my improvisation may well contain bits borrowed from Parker or Pass.

Thus, improvisation is far less spontaneous, far less singular, and far more interpretive than we might at first assume. But this is the case with any *technē*. For, in practicing a skill, even if the goal of that practice is a pure repetition, what actually results is never pure. There is always the change of improvisation present. An apprentice of a cabinet maker may well start by copying ("interpreting") the master craftsman but almost certainly will end up making cabinets that have modifications (however small) of his own – improvising. Conversely, while a given improvisation will undoubtedly have certain unique features, it cannot be seen as a *purely* unique creation.

In any case, improvisation is based not only on a score but on an entire performance tradition that is always present to some degree in every improvisation. Most performances and improvisations are (at least usually) "readings" or interpretations of scores, even if those scores and what it means to "read" them may differ significantly in respective cases. Even to play a piece based on an unwritten tradition is to improvise and interpret. Thus, an improvisation is never simply a presentation: it is always a kind of *re*presentation. In that sense, improvisation can be seen as a kind of performance.

On the other hand, we can just as easily turn this around. We have already seen that – given the *Unbestimmtheitsstellen* of musical works – performers cannot help but be improvisers. So to what extent is performance a kind of presentation of something new in the sense of improvisation? In the same way that it is impossible to construe improvisation solely in terms of presentation, it is likewise impossible to interpret performance solely in terms of representation: for a performance necessarily requires improvisation if it is to exist at all. Admittedly, the classical performer bent on fidelity to the score is almost assuredly improvising a great deal less than someone playing a jazz tune. Of course, given admissions of early music performers as to how much they were simply "making up" as they went along, one should be careful not to underemphasize the improvisation present in those performances. But, from what we have seen in previous chapters, it should be clear at this point that the difference is far more quantitative than qualitative. True, whereas the jazz musician has no qualms about changing even such basics as the melody or harmony, the classical musician is likely going to be making more limited changes such as tempi or dynamics. Of course, we also have seen that performers of classical music – both past and present – have also changed notes or dropped measures, as they saw fit. In the end, then, we might say that perhaps the most significant difference is that, whereas in jazz a musician improvises freely and openly, in classical music the requirement of fidelity has meant that the improvisational element has, to a great extent, been suppressed – or else has operated covertly.

But, if even performance is inherently the introduction of something that goes beyond the score *and* is necessary for a piece of music to *exist*, then a piece of music has an identity that inevitably changes. In other words, the musical work might best be described by precisely the definition Ingarden rejects: "an object enduring in historical time that slowly, yet inevitably changes." What would it mean to rethink the *ergon* as *energeia* – an activity that "lives" and "grows" into a kind of structure that develops an identity?

Dwelling Musically

We saw in Chapters 2 and 3 that composing and performing represent a multipart invention, one that depends on that which has gone before and that takes shape within the improvisatory movement of performance. Thus, the identity of musical pieces is always in motion. Composition does not represent a "break-off point," in the same way that it was not a pure "beginning point" of that process. Instead, what we call a "work" might better be thought of as a developing structure that arises from the activity of music making.

Although Heidegger clearly has the concept of "work" (and not "piece") in mind when he speaks of the "work of art" as opening up a "world," I think Heidegger's conception here actually exemplifies the concept of "piece" rather than "work." Note that even human beings (what Heidegger calls "Dasein") are such that they always go with a world. Indeed, human beings and their environments are linked together in such a way that one could never *be* without the other. To use Heideggerian language, Dasein is "*in-der-Welt-sein*" (being-in-the-world), since Dasein "dwells" within its world. Here Heidegger should not be read as giving us a spatial metaphor: we are not in the world as water in a glass. Rather, the world provides the horizon for existence.[32] Thus, "world" as Heidegger uses it does not mean a totality of physical objects but a "home" in which we live. Of course, there are multiple and overlapping worlds in which we dwell, and we can move in and out of them.

If we say (modifying Heidegger) that a piece of music opens up a world, it should be clear this "world" of the piece of music is one that is not self-contained. Rather, it is a world within a world, a musical space that is created *within* and *out of* a larger musical practice. Moreover, just as the world of Dasein is not a *physical* world but a world of activity, so the piece of music is likewise a world of activity. It is a "space" that is both created by and allows for musical activity. But what does it mean for a performer to exist within this space? Of course, in one sense, the answer is obvious. If composers improvise their pieces amid the activity of music making, then performers are *already there.* For they are just as much a part of music making as composers. *There is no sense in which the composer is prior* – either ontologically or historically. But, since new worlds known as musical pieces

[32] Martin Heidegger, *Being and Time*, trans. John Jacquarrie and Edward Robinson (New York: Harper & Row, 1962) ¶12.

come to be amidst the worlds of music (and there are many worlds of music), so performers take on special roles regarding these new worlds. As Heidegger recognizes, the existence of the space created by a piece of music is equally dependent on both its creators and preservers: "Just as a work cannot be without being created but is essentially in need of creators, so what is created cannot itself come into being without those who preserve it." But what does it mean to be a *preserver* of this musical clearing? Heidegger characterizes preservation in terms of "standing within the openness" that the piece of music creates.[33] To stand within the openness, of course, is not to preserve in the sense of a museum-like preservation. Rather, the act of dwelling within that space is simultaneously the act of transforming it into a musical habitation. And, as we noted in Chapter 1, this musical sort of dwelling is characterized not only by improvisation but also by "improvement."

But in what sense might improvisation prove to be a sort of "improving"? Is it possible to maintain that the improvising activity that takes place in performance represents a genuine improvement, so that a jazz tune, a chorale by Bach, or a folk song can truly be said to be "bettered"? One thing is clear: whatever "improvement" improvisation can be said to bring about cannot be defined in terms of anything like "an ever-better interpretation," any more than we can see the history of music as animated by an invisible hand of progress. Yet, improvement need not be defined in simplistic normative terms. The original meanings of "improve" convey a very different idea, one not necessarily connected with making anything "better" in the sense of "progressively better." In its original sense, improvement has to do with the way in which we relate to our surroundings, so that "improve" can be defined as: "To turn (a thing) to profit or good

[33] "The Origin of the Work of Art" 66 and 47.

account."[34] Traditionally, improvement has often been associated with the cultivation of land: to live on the land means "improving" that land in the sense of enhancing and nourishing it so that it yields an abundant harvest. Cultivating the land is a way of dwelling in a place, but a way in which one becomes a part of that place and makes that place into a home. Thus, any increase in merit or value that this improvement brings about can be defined only in relation to those who dwell within that space. While it may be possible to talk about a kind of "progress" that dwelling brings about, that progress is more like the kind about which Wittgenstein speaks – the kind that comes from scratching an existing itch.[35] It is a kind of progress that can only be defined in light of actual needs, not theoretical ideals. The musical improviser, then, is always engaged in making the music say something to and be useful for *us*, in the same way that future improvisers will be engaged in making music that says something to and is useful for those who come after.

Yet, might not there be some wider and more significant sense in which a piece of music can be said to be "improved"? Given that the piece of music receives its full identity in being performed, the identity of a piece of music is constantly in the state of being improvised. Thus, its identity comes to be over time, being defined by the succession of improvised performances that actually take place. Thus, one may dwell *within* the space created by a piece of music, but the act of dwelling always means that one is always to some extent – even if small or imperceptible – dwelling *at the limits* of the space and transgressing those limits. Dwelling inherently involves adding on, replacing, and altering.

---

[34] See *The Oxford English Dictionary*, 2nd ed., s.v. "improve."

[35] "Philosophy hasn't made any progress? – If somebody scratches the spot where he has an itch, do we have to see some progress?" See Ludwig Wittgenstein, *Culture and Value*, trans. Peter Winch, ed. G. H. von Wright (Oxford: Basil Blackwell, 1980) no. 86e.

There is a sense, then, in which musical dwelling is always on the edge: for dwelling always involves both the exploration of the boundaries of a given piece and musical practice and also the modification of those boundaries. And that practice also serves to shape – at least in some respects – the boundaries or limits of the musical piece. While the space that a piece of music creates is a kind of context in which music can happen, that context is itself a *dependent* one – not something autonomous. Like composition, performance hovers around the limits of the musical space created by the piece – both respecting them and altering them (which can also be a way of "respecting" them). That altering, of course, can be appropriate or inappropriate, welcome or unwelcome, tasteful or tasteless, useful or useless – but it cannot be absent.

In the end, our conception of a piece of music (which is to say: the piece of music *itself*) is formed through the interplay of identity and difference between scores, performances, and our continually developing "conceptions" of a work. In this respect, it is significant that Stravinsky regarded his recordings (to quote him) "*as indispensable supplements to the printed music.*"[36] The history of the coming-to-be of a piece of music is a multipart invention and a *continuing* invention, from the very first stage of the composition process until not only the piece is no longer being performed but all vestiges of it have passed from memory.

When Stravinsky says that his recordings can be taken as supplements to the score, this can be understood in at least three different senses. First, "supply" carries the idea of making something complete. Neither the idea in the composer's head nor the notes on the page are in any way an actualized piece of music; instead, their fruition comes about in the performance. So performance is a kind of completion of the musical piece, making it

---

[36] *Conversations with Igor Stravinsky* 119 (my italics).

truly "real." Should a piece never be performed, in this important sense, it never becomes "real." Second, the supplemental action of the performance is also a kind of alteration. In being performed, the performance adds to both the idea in the composer's head and the score. Thus, our ideas of what constitutes "Brahms" are shaped by what we have actually *heard*; and, while we can always refer anew to the score (and perhaps even discover some account that the composer had given long ago as to "what he had in mind"), that score is always read in terms of the score-as-heard, which is to say the score-as-supplemented-by-the-performance.

Third, and perhaps the most important way in which the musical dwelling of performance affects the work within which it dwells, is that of *enrichment*.[37] Thus, Bach's *St. Matthew Passion* is not just an idea, not just a score, not just an original performance in the Thomaskirche in Leipzig, not just Mendelssohn's romantic reconstruction of it in 1829, nor even just the reconstructed versions that have become popular in the past few decades. It is all of these, and also more than merely the sum total of those parts. And it is through the improvisatory movement of the supplements that a piece of music can be said to be "improved" in the sense of being *augmented*. Whereas an idea or a score is merely potential music, the actualization that comes about by way of performances increases its being. That is not to say that there is no loss involved: for the fact that performances are in some sense replacements means that some aspects that have been previously actualized are lost. Yet, since pieces of music can be not only constantly improvised but also preserved both in memory

---

[37] Even a performance that one might be inclined to term an "impoverishment" (given its poor quality or the inability of musicians to "follow the score" – however one might construe that) is *still* an "enrichment." For the performance is now connected to the piece in some sense and so makes it "greater" (ontologically, even if not aesthetically).

and – now – by way of recording, there is clearly a net increase of possibilities that comes about.

A particularly poignant example of the supplementation by performance can be seen in the history of Thelonious Monk's tune "Round Midnight" composed in 1944. When it was first recorded by Cootie Williams, he felt free (as would most jazz musicians) to embellish the melody. But those embellishments were then picked up by the sheet music versions, since they were based on the recording rather than something written. Then, when Dizzie Gillespie recorded it in 1946, he included both an introduction and a coda that originally had been part of his standard rendition of "I Can't Get Started." Those changes so affected the identity of "Round Midnight" that Monk *himself* adopted them. By the time Miles Davis recorded the tune in 1955, not only did he follow the by-then "standard" changes but also included three new measures at the end of the first chorus (as a kind of interlude).[38] The result is that, today, *all* of those embellishments have become part of the identity of "Round Midnight." Here we are not talking about *harmonic* changes that jazz musicians make routinely but about the very "melody itself."

Whereas a performance does actualize a piece of music in sound, that actualization is itself open to being revised by subsequent performances. In other words, pieces of music would seem to remain just that: pieces that are never fully defined and always in the process of being defined. Is a piece of music, then, characterized by what Gadamer (following Hegel) considers the "bad infinite" – that is, an infinite succession (at least in principle) in which there is no sense of completion? There is an important sense in which a performance *does* bring a piece of music to a real kind of completion: in being performed a piece is no longer merely "potential" music and its places of indeterminacy

---

[38] See *Thinking in Jazz* 88.

(although perhaps not *all* of its places of indeterminacy) are by necessity made determinate. But this completion is in no way a final, once-for-all completion. Thus, musical pieces are constantly in the process of being completed, but it is a completion that arrives only to be superseded – again and again.

On Musical Identity

Is there some way of conceiving the relationship between the piece and the performance that does not subordinate either the *ergon* to the *energeia* – or vice versa?

On the one hand, as long as we think of pieces of music as being "works" with an ideal existence, we are inclined to overlook or else downplay the role of the performance. If music is truly sound, though, then performances cannot *simply* disappear into the work because – without them – there is nothing to slip into. On the other hand, if performances also *present* the piece and continue to develop it, then it is likewise impossible for the piece to disappear into the performance. Thus, the piece and the performance would seem to be *essentially* connected to one another. After hearing a particular performance, we may comment on the piece that was performed or the performance itself; but we cannot experience the piece apart from the performance or the performance apart from the piece. Thus, performances are at once emissaries *and* also part of what they represent, in the same way that Merleau-Ponty says that "expression is everywhere creative."[39]

The result is that the identity of a piece of music can only be grasped *as it unfolds and continues to unfold.* The identity of a piece

[39] Maurice Merleau-Ponty, *Phenomenology of Perception*, trans. Colin Smith (London: Routledge & Kegan Paul, 1962) 391.

of music comes at the end, not at the beginning. Since pieces of music are never static, their identity is – like any other thing that is alive and growing – one that never reaches a point of complete definition. Nietzsche rightly points out that "only that which has no history is definable."[40] Anything that is alive is not yet ready to be defined. However, whereas performances are never *identical* either to the piece or to one another, they are still *identifiable* with both.

But, if the history of a piece of music is at least partly a history of its supplements, what accounts for the identity of a piece of music? Clearly, musical identity is not based on any *one* thing; rather it is established by a complex set of factors and the interaction of those factors. And this makes copyright infringement cases difficult.[41] Thus, many of those factors – including even portions of the melody – can be changed without causing it to lose its identity, even if it is no longer an unchanging identity. Exactly how many of these factors could be changed and the piece still retain its identity is a question that can be answered only on the basis of specific examples; and, in more difficult cases, we may well have trouble reaching agreement. On the other hand, there can be remarkable similarities between what we take to be "different" pieces, without any identity crisis.

The problem of musical identity is (as we will see shortly) remarkably similar to human identity. But it is also more complicated. For, whereas our judgments of personal identity are restricted to either positive or negative ones (that is, one is either the same person or not – there is an excluded middle),

[40] Friedrich Nietzsche, *On the Genealogy of Morality*, trans. Maudmarie Clark and Alan J. Swensen (Indianapolis: Hackett, 1998) Second Treatise, §13 (p.53).
[41] Of course, such cases do not hinge merely on similarity but (and more important) *access*. To win, a plaintiff must show that the performer/recording company had access to the piece.

those concerning pieces of music have a much greater range of possibility – and thus ambiguity and room for conflicting intuitions. Performances, arrangements, transcriptions, and orchestrations can be done with the aim of scrupulous fidelity – or with a free hand. Does, for instance, a "faithful" transcription count as the same piece, whereas a more "free" transcription is to be classified as a separate entity? On Davies's account, "a transcription must depart far enough from the original to count as a distinct piece." But, as sensible as that requirement sounds, what exactly would constitute "far enough"? Davies is right that "one does not transcribe a harpsichord concerto merely by crossing out the word 'harpsichord' on the score and replacing it with the word 'piano'." Yet, would crossing out the word "harpsichord" and replacing it with "accordion" count as a transcription then? All three instruments have keyboards and all can play chords. But is there enough of a difference between an accordion and a harpsichord? On the other hand, what counts as "too far"? Davies likewise stipulates that "it is a necessary condition for transcription that the musical content of the transcriber's score should adequately resemble and preserve the musical content of the original work."[42] The problem with this stipulation is not so much the requirement that a transcription "resemble" the original work – for clearly some sense of "resemblance" is necessary in all cases of transcriptions, orchestrations, arrangements, and even most performances – but that this resemblance be "adequate." Clearly, "adequacy" depends here on the degree of preservation of "musical content." But the *degree* of "musical content" that is necessary for there to be anything like "resemblance" is precisely what is so difficult to specify, whether we are talking about performance, arrangement, orchestration or transcription.

[42] Stephen Davies, "Transcription, Authenticity and Performance," *British Journal of Aesthetics* 28 (1988) 216–17.

Suppose, going back to the example of Beethoven's *Hammerklavier Sonata* considered in Chapter 3, we were to play it on a modern piano, exchange the Adagio for the Scherzo (and vice versa), and omit the introduction to the Fugue. Most people (though perhaps not all) would agree that we were listening to the "same" piece (the question here being one not of aesthetic quality but simply ontological identity). But, suppose further, that we were to shorten some of the movements (perhaps even severely) and tinker with some of the notes (perhaps reasoning that "Beethoven probably would (or should) have changed these, if he had just gotten around to it"), would it still be the "same"? For most listeners, the verdict would probably be that the two "pieces" were not identical but could be *identified* with one another. Obviously, such an example could be pushed much further and in different ways: random motifs of the *Hammerklavier Sonata* performed by kazoo band or improvisations on some sections of the piece but not others or portions of the piece "spliced" with portions of other Beethoven pieces (using, say, techniques found in rap music).[43]

Jazz improvisations complicate the matter far more, for so much can be changed (in spite of whatever tune might be listed in the program notes). In any case, what counts as identity in jazz is inevitably going to be different from identity as defined in classical music, for their respective senses of identity are highly dependent on the specific discourses that set their limitations. What would count in jazz as still being the same may well be taken to be

---

[43] Note that these examples are not quite as far-fetched as they might seem. Charles Rosen points out that "the premiere of Beethoven's violin concerto was made more interesting by the interpolation between the first and second movements of a sonata for upside-down violin with one string, written by the violinist." As Rosen goes on to say, "this is only the most scandalous and bizarre example of a general tradition." See Charles Rosen, "Should Music Be Played Wrong?" *High Fidelity* (May 1971) 55.

a wholly different entity from the perspective of classical music. And these identity questions have only gotten more difficult (and are sure to become *continually* more difficult) in an age of technology in which rap pieces contain "samplings" from 1970s rock songs and Natalie Cole sings with her father Nat.[44] Of course, these problems of identity can certainly be overemphasized. Practically speaking, musical performances can exhibit a great deal of *identity* without being *identical*. Thus, pieces undoubtedly change, but they *usually* retain an identity, certainly enough for the practical purposes of identification. Indeed, what is perhaps most amazing is how much a piece can be altered – purposely or not – and still remain more or less recognizable. When Goodman worries that "if we allow the *least deviation* [from the score], all assurance of work-preservation and score-preservation is lost" and "we can go all the way from Beethoven's *Fifth Symphony* to *Three Blind Mice*," we shouldn't worry along with him.[45]

However strange these problems of musical identity may seem, they really aren't so strange after all. For we have the same sorts of identity difficulties with human persons, who are also living entities. If, for example, we encounter someone who is aged or altered in appearance, certain aspects of that person may cause us to wonder if we are seeing the "same" person, even though other aspects may remain unchanged. Thus, we sometimes have conflicting intuitions: the voice sounds roughly the same, for example, but the face is markedly altered (or perhaps vice versa). While we might not even recognize the person at first, after listening to the voice and looking more carefully at the face we may decide that it is the "same" person after all (although we may well make this decision and, at the same time, say "he's changed").

[44] One must not forget, though, that the identity problems of "sampling" or "quotation" are found in pieces by Charles Ives, not to mention the examples we noted in Handel.

[45] *Languages of Art* 186–7 (my italics).

Thus, while such a statement as "You're not the same as you used to be" might well be perceived as offensive (we usually prefer "you haven't changed a bit," even if the person is lying), it can be said meaningfully. In this case, "you" are an entity that is perceived to be in some important sense "the same" *and* in another important sense "different." And it is precisely the continuity that allows the speaker to make the observation that "you" have changed. There is no magical way in which the speaker has determined this. Instead, there is simply the appeal to a variety of factors that allow the speaker to construe you as you. Even if we *were* to argue that what ultimately makes you you is an "essence" or something similar, it would be hard to argue that the speaker had access to that essence and, on the basis of that access, determined that you were you.[46]

Given the similar problems of identity of musical pieces and human persons, we could – following Wittgenstein's suggestion – say that our perception of identity is much like our perception of family resemblances: as Wittgenstein puts it, family members "are *related* to one another in many different ways."[47] Despite Goodman's insistence that one wrong note in a performance discounts it from being an "instance" of a particular piece, we actually judge various incarnations of a piece of music to instantiate the "same" piece if they have a kind of family resemblance rather than strict identity. Just as people may differ in judging whether a newborn child really "looks like" her mother or father (or grandmother or grandfather), so we may not always agree on the extent to which, say, a transcription is more like a "copy"

---

[46] See the discussion in Peter Strawson, *Individuals* (London: Methuen, 1957) and, more recently, Paul Ricoeur, *Oneself as Another*, trans. Kathleen Blamey (Chicago: The University of Chicago Press, 1992) 27–39.

[47] Ludwig Wittgenstein, *Philosophical Investigations: Revised German-English Translation*, ed. Elizabeth Anscombe (Oxford: Blackwell, 2002) nos. 65 and 67.

of a given work or is instead like a "different" work. And, most of the time, such disagreements turn out to be of relatively minor import. Usually, they become important for "nonaesthetic" reasons (when enormous amounts of money are at stake, for example).

Acknowledging that musical pieces are growing, changing entities in no way means that we need to give up the notion of authorial intent. On the one hand, Hirsch is right in insisting that the meaning of a text (or score) is tied to the author's will or intention. Pieces of music do not come about merely by accident and any given piece will have imbedded in it the intentions (whether low-level, middle-level, or high-level) of the composer. Of course, part of being a competent composer is learning how to notate those intentions, and composers will have varying degrees of success in that regard. On the other hand, when Beardsley claims that "texts acquire determinate meaning through the interactions of their words" he is likewise right.[48] In fact, texts do not simply acquire meaning through the interaction of words (or, in this case, notes) but also through interaction with performance traditions – past, present, and future. Where he goes wrong is in adding the phrase "without the intervention of an authorial will." True, the composer cannot merely "intervene" in decreeing what performers must do (though composers like Stravinsky have certainly *tried*). But merely the act of writing a score (or, for that matter, playing a riff) represents the expression of an intention.

One last question concerning the "identity" of a piece of music remains. What comes first – the activity or the structure? Such a question is considerably more difficult to answer than it might at first seem. Obviously, it makes little sense – given all that we have seen so far – to say that music making arose from pieces

---

[48] *Intention and Interpretation* 31–2.

of music. I have argued that musical practices are precisely the basis from which pieces of music arise. Yet, if we begin with music making, then *what music* was being made in that activity? In other words, which forms the possibility conditions for the other? I think the answer here – to both the historical and the logical forms of this question – is that pieces of music simply are *synonymous* with musical practice. Of course, "works" certainly aren't synonymous with musical practice. For there was music making long before anyone had coined the concept "work." However, on my view, there also are no "works," at least in the sense of self-contained, autonomous entities. *There have always only been pieces*, despite whatever our theories have proclaimed. And that applies to Kern's "All the Things You Are" or Bach's *St. Matthew Passion* or Tchaikovsky's Sixth Symphony. In other words, the "structures" that we call pieces of music are "composed" of the activity of music making itself, rather than music making "plus some other thing" (that we would call a "work").

Oddly enough, on my view, whether composers were working with the "work concept" *does* make a difference, in one sense. But not because they – in so thinking and designating ("I hereby christen thee a work") – actually create a "work." Rather, in thinking that this is what they are doing, the *activity* of music making is affected. For confirmation, one need only consider the existence of concert halls and the rituals that go with them. Or the music editor trying to discover the *Fassung letzter Hand*. Clearly, musical activity *has* been affected by the work concept. But, as I have argued all along, musical activity has only been *somewhat* altered by the ideals of "composer as true creator" and *Werktreue*. Performers have always found ways to be part of the creative process, even when they thought they were doing the exact opposite. Practice and theory, of course, are often out of step.

To someone who might counter by saying "But weren't there first scales and arpeggios and the like before there were pieces," my answer would be: not likely. For, while we know remarkably little about the beginnings of *truly* ancient music (by which I mean not the sort of thing that Bach would have heard but the sort of thing that, say, Homer would have heard), it seems implausible that anyone first decided to play scales and then discovered that one could form pieces out of them. So it seems to me that there have always been pieces. And musical activity has always been centered around them – and still is.

Having shown that pieces of music are thoroughly grounded in musical activity, we need to consider what it means to be part of the community of music makers.

FIVE

Being Musical with the Other

Of all instrumental music, [a string quartet] is for me the most comprehensible: one hears four rational persons conversing with each other, and believes that one gains something from their discourse and becomes acquainted with the peculiarities of their instruments.[1]

A STRING QUARTET WOULD AT LEAST *SEEM* TO BE A KIND OF musical conversation. In playing a quartet, each member contributes to the discourse; and their contributions give the impression of forming a mutual exchange. But this immediately raises a crucial question: if a string quartet can be termed a kind of dialogue, *who is speaking?* Goethe implies that we hear the players themselves in conversation; but are their voices really their own? Do they speak for themselves or do they speak merely on behalf of the composer? What sorts of obligations do composers, performers, and listeners have to their dialogical others? And how is it possible to blend these voices into a genuine dialogue in which no voice is simply absorbed or drowned out by any of the others

[1] Johann Wolfgang von Goethe, in a letter to Karl Friedrich Zelter (November 9, 1829). See *Goethes Briefe* (Hamburg: Christian Wegner, 1967) Vol. IV, 349.

and the particularities of their respective voices are allowed to flourish?

Since music making is something that we inevitably do with others (whether they are present or not), musical dialogue is *fundamentally* ethical in nature. But, for there to be a genuine dialogue, then *neither* the composer(s) *nor* the performer(s) *nor* the listener(s) can be so dominant that the other voices are simply forgotten. Whereas interpretational theories that emphasize "authorial intention" clearly give undue weight to authors and composers, there is the opposite danger of giving privilege to performers or listeners. Is there a way of doing justice to each voice?

The Voice of the Other

No philosophical figure in the past century has been more adamant in arguing against the tendency to suppress the voice of the other than Emmanuel Levinas, who claims precisely that "philosophy consists in suppressing or transmuting the alterity of all that is Other."[2] Of course, philosophers are hardly alone in being guilty of not taking the other seriously or simply disregarding the other all together. The model of the artistic genius sketched by Kant gives us the epitome of the lone individual who wants nothing less than to speak in such a way as to supplant all other voices.

Behind this suppression of otherness, thinks Levinas, is a desire for autonomy. Certainly, this has been the case in art. It is no accident that Kant gives us both the model of the free artistic genius and also a conception of morality in which autonomy is

[2] Emmanuel Levinas, "Transcendence and Height," in *Basic Philosophical Writings*, ed. Adriaan Peperzak, Simon Critchley, and Robert Bernasconi (Bloomington: Indiana University Press, 1996) 11.

central. For Kant, it is only when one acts on the basis of one's own reason that one is truly free. And it is only when the artistic genius is unfettered that true works of genius can result. Levinas too sees the move toward autonomy as designed to create a space for personal freedom. But, while for Kant this freedom is positive, for Levinas it is deeply disturbing. For my freedom comes at the expense of the other's freedom, my own autonomous world at the expense of the other's heteronomy. Whereas Kant sees freedom in primarily negative terms (that is, I am "free" when not constrained by another), Levinas welcomes the constraint of the other. Of course, since the other (at least on Levinas's account) is *infinitely* other, that otherness can never really be destroyed, even though it certainly can be ignored, denied, and compromised.

Yet, how is the "autonomous monologue" to be avoided so that a true dialogue can be maintained? At this point, one might be inclined to suggest that the answer to *Werktreue* (however construed) might be the kind of existentialist "authenticity" associated with Kierkegaard, Heidegger, or Sartre.[3] But these two sorts of authenticity end up being mirror images of one another. And so they go wrong in exactly the same way.

Instead of acting as the "middleman," in the more romantic performance tradition, a common piece of advice given to performers has tended to be along the lines of "make the piece your own." This is remarkably similar to the notion of *Eigentlichkeit* in Heidegger. To be *eigentlich* for Heidegger is not simply to be "authentic" but to "be yourself." Now, in one sense, both of these bits of advice – "make it your own" and "be yourself" – are perfectly sensible, and even desirable. One of the difficulties that performers have in approaching a piece of music that is

---

[3] Such is the course suggested by, for instance, Bruce Baugh, "Authenticity Revisited," *Journal of Aesthetics and Art Criticism* 46 (1988) 477–87. Also see Peter Kivy, *Authenticities: Philosophical Reflections on Musical Performance* (Ithaca, N.Y.: Cornell University Press, 1995) 108–42.

unfamiliar (especially if it is in an unfamiliar style) is that it is difficult to "feel at home" with the piece. It is hardly possible to play something very well – and certainly not to play something *convincingly* – if it feels simply alien and strange. So "making the piece one's own" and "being oneself" are in some sense *necessary* to a good performance.

Yet, the problem is that the structure of *Eigentlichkeit* is all too close to that of Kant's autonomy. When Heidegger says that "understanding is either authentic, *arising out of one's own Self as such*, or inauthentic," it is hard to distinguish this sense of authenticity from Kant's account of autonomy.[4] For, in both cases, the self is not merely supposed to be the *principal* but the *sole* determining factor. In place of the monologue of the composer, we now have the monologue of the performer. And, of course, if the listener takes this same stance, then we have yet a different monologue. If we consider the history of the romantic performance tradition, it is not hard to see that the response to the heavy-handed composer often has been a counterattack by way of an equally heavy-handed performer. Both Lizst and Paganini popularized a "virtuoso tradition" in which audiences came to hear *them*, as much as (or even *more than*) the pieces they were playing (and those pieces were often conveniently altered to show off their remarkable virtuosity). Of course, remnants of that tradition continued into the twentieth century, particularly as some conductors came to see *themselves* as the true creators.

In contrast, then, to privileging the composer, the performer, or the listener, Levinas is right in saying that "to approach the Other is to put into question my freedom, my spontaneity."[5] And

---

[4] *Being and Time* 186 (my italics). Incidentally, Heidegger borrows the notion of authenticity from Kierkegaard, and then Sartre appropriates it from Heidegger.
[5] Emmanuel Levinas, *Totality and Infinity*, trans. Alphonso Lingus (The Hague: Martinus Nijhoff, 1979) 303.

that works in all directions. When Leonard Bernstein says that "perhaps the chief requirement of all is that [the conductor] be humble before the composer," he is only partly right.[6] Humility is indeed an appropriate stance of the performer. But it is likewise an appropriate stance of the composer. And an appropriate stance of the listener. The "ideal" composer, performer, or listener is one who is really ready to encounter an other who (as Gadamer puts it) "breaks into my ego-centeredness and gives me something to understand."[7] To treat the other *as other* requires that I recognize the other as having a kind of claim on me. Naturally, the kind of claim and the force of that claim depend upon the specific dialogue, for dialogues can be of different sorts and even musical dialogues differ. Yet, to take the other seriously means that I am not simply "free" to do "whatever I please."

But, then, what sort of freedom *do* I have? And, more important, what sort of responsibility does the other *have to me*? Levinas steadfastly refuses to answer this second question, for a very simple reason. The danger of the logic of reciprocity is that (among other things) a reciprocal dialogue can easily degenerate into a monologue in which one party dictates the conditions of "reciprocity." The composer can say, for instance: "As long as you faithfully follow my instructions, you are participating in a true dialogue." But the performer is hardly immune from responding: "No, a true dialogue with you (and "you" can be defined as either composer or text or both) instead must take the form of a creative reworking in which the score merely serves as the springboard for my own musical genius."

[6] Leonard Bernstein, *The Joy of Music* (New York: Simon and Schuster, 1959) 151.
[7] Hans-Georg Gadamer, "Reflections on My Philosophical Journey," in *The Philosophy of Hans-Georg Gadamer*, ed. Lewis Edwin Hahn (Chicago: Open Court, 1997) 46.

Clearly, though, *some* sense of reciprocity is necessary for a musical dialogue. So what form might that reciprocity take in order to keep the dialogue from degenerating into a monologue? I think the answer – to whatever extent there can be anything like an "answer" to such a question – is that reciprocity, to put it one way, "always begins at home." Gadamer insists that "good will" is absolutely necessary for understanding between one another. For Gadamer, "good will" is demonstrated not when one attempts "to prove that one is always right" but when "one seeks instead as far as possible to strengthen the other's viewpoint so that what the other person has to say becomes illuminating."[8] *If* there is to be anything resembling reciprocity, *then* it must begin with me. True reciprocity is only possible if I make the first move – without knowing that the other will reciprocate. Of course, whether I am a composer, performer, or listener, making the first move makes me vulnerable. For there is no guarantee that you (or anyone else taking part in the dialogue) will reciprocate. But there is no way around this danger.

Yet, once that move is made, what then? In order to explain how the other and I can relate, Gadamer uses the metaphor of a "fusion of horizons." In one sense, this notion is a helpful way of thinking about this encounter. On Gadamer's account, successful communication takes place when the "horizon" (or perspective) of the listener "fuses" (or, perhaps better, "connects") with that of the performer, composer, and tradition. The score and/or composer has one sort of horizon (temporally, culturally, musically, and perhaps otherwise) and performers and listeners have yet other horizons. The goal, then, is a "fusion" of these horizons to enable a genuine dialogue. The horizon, say, of Bach's

---

[8] "Reply to Jacques Derrida," in *Dialogue and Deconstruction: The Gadamer-Derrida Encounter*, ed. Diane P. Michelfelder and Richard E. Palmer (Albany: State University of New York Press, 1989) 55.

St. Matthew Passion becomes connected to ours, so that there is some kind of mutuality – one might say a communion. And, since the horizons of performers and listeners are constantly in motion, new (and thus different) fusions can (and do) continually take place.

But the danger of this metaphor of "fusion" of horizons (in German, *Horizontverschmelzung*) is that – in "fusing" with the other – the "otherness" of the other is lost. And such a danger is hardly a theoretical problem, one that could be fixed merely by substituting a new metaphor. *Verschmelzen* can be defined as "to melt into one another" and the result of such a *Verschmelzung* – or at least a possible result – is the loss of distinctive voices. No doubt, the goal of, say, a given choral performance might well be that the literal voices "meld" so that they sound as one (though, if they are singing particular *parts*, a complete melding would be undesirable). Yet, clearly the goal – even in such a performance – is not that the identities of respective performers is simply lost. Rather, the goal is to find some kind of blend that does not simply erase particular identity. As we noted in Chapter 3, it is all too easy to impose our *own* horizon and then proclaim it as the "authentic" horizon of the past. To be honest, performers *always* face this reality. The goal of the composer, performer, and listener seeking a genuine dialogue, then, is both to be aware of this danger and to be creative in allowing each party to have a real voice. And, of course, there is an important sense in which the danger of a "fusion of horizons" is mitigated. Since my horizon is never truly "mine" (given that I am part of a culture – both musically and in general – that I do not possess and cannot control), then "my" horizon is always a shared horizon and so is *always* affected by otherness.

Assuming that some sort of "connection" is made between the composer/composition and the performer (and thus the audience), then how is the composer's voice able to be heard?

Although the idea of allowing music to "speak for itself" has been an important regulative ideal of classical music (for it is closely connected to the ideal of *Werktreue*), music has no existence apart from the voices of the conversation. However worthy this ideal may sound, it is simply impossible. In effect, the performer acts as the representative of the composer – and also of the musical tradition. Although Gadamer is here writing about texts in general, what he says applies to musical texts as well: "One partner in the hermeneutical conversation, the text, speaks only through the other partner, the interpreter."[9] A text can only *mean* by way of the act of interpretation and a score can only *sound* through a performance. And this applies equally to folk music that has never been written, for such music can only *sound* by way of a performer who brings it to voice. But that in no ways means that the interpreter simply (as Gadamer puts it in a later text) "disappears – and the text speaks."[10] For, in speaking on behalf of the composer (and the musical tradition), the performer does not simply *disappear*.

How, then, should we think of this relationship? I think the way in which stringed instruments are tuned provides an important clue. Alfred Schutz speaks of a "mutual tuning-in relationship" between those making and listening to music.[11] And that "tuning" depends on a kind of tension. In the same way that instruments are tuned on the basis of tension, so the relationship of musical partners depends on tension to be maintained. On the one hand, as composer or performer or listener I open myself to the other when I feel the pull of the other that demands my respect. On the other hand, my openness to the other cannot be

9 *Truth and Method* 387.
10 "Text and Interpretation," in *Dialogue and Deconstruction* 51.
11 Alfred Schutz, "Making Music Together" in *Collected Papers II, Studies in Social Theory*, ed. Arvid Brodersen (The Hague: Martinus Nijhoff, 1964) 73.

simply a complete giving in to the other, for then I am no longer myself and am instead simply absorbed by the other. Thus, a dialogue can only be maintained if there is a pull exerted by both sides. The danger for genuine dialogue, then, is not the *presence* of tension but its loss or imbalance. A dialogue is only possible when each partner *both* holds the others in tension – that is, holds the other accountable – *and* feels the tension of accountability exerted by the other. As strange as it may sound, these "tensions" actually make the "freedom" of dialogue possible. Why that sounds strange is because we usually think of freedom as "negative freedom" – freedom *from* constraints. But what I have in mind here is "positive freedom" – freedom *for* genuine dialogue. Of course, in order to "feel that pull," one needs to be able to *listen* to the other.[12]

While it is relatively easy to see that we are obliged to fellow performers, listeners, and living composers, why are we obliged to composers who are no longer living and the tradition in general? On my view, tradition is never simply an "it," for traditions are highly dependent on those who have gone before us. So respecting traditions involves respecting people (which means that answering the first question answers the second). I think most of us would readily concede that we have a responsibility even to those no longer in our midst, though there is no unanimous agreement on this issue. Dipert argues, for instance, that "we have very little, if any, moral obligations to [dead composers]."[13] Whether someone is a composer is clearly not the primary issue, of course. As long as we assume that we owe human others a certain respect and that this obligation does not simply perish in

---

[12] F. J. Smith, *The Experiencing of Musical Sound: Prelude to a Phenomenology of Music* (New York: Gordon and Breach, 1979) 17.

[13] "The Composer's Intentions: An Examination of their Relevance for Performance" 213.

death, then that obligation continues to have *some* claim on us.[14] If Hirsch is right that "speech is an extension and expression of men in the social domain," then we owe a certain respect to the words and works of even dead authors and composers precisely because we owe a certain respect to authors and composers themselves.[15] Since I take that obligation as a given, my concern here is *how that obligation is to be worked out in practice.*

We have seen that pieces of music are neither autonomous from the musical context nor autonomous from the composer. While composers can never be taken to be the *sole* authors of the compositions that bear their names (since they are always indebted to so many others), those compositions are still expressions that strongly bear the composer's "imprint." P. D. Juhl points out that even appeals to the text or context when attempting to argue for one's interpretation are usually appeals, often implicit, to the author's.[16] By way of writing (whether a literary text or a score – or, for that matter, a phenomenology of music) the author in some sense "participates" in the ensuing dialogue. Most authors feel a connection to their texts and are concerned for their fate, even if they may differ as to just how closely they identify with their texts (and how much they care what performers do with them).[17] And most performers recognize that same sense of connection.

---

[14] Kivy takes a similar position to mine but for different reasons. See his essay "Live Performances and Dead Composers," in *The Fine Art of Repetition* 106–8.

[15] E. D. Hirsch, Jr., *The Aims of Interpretation* (Chicago: University of Chicago Press, 1976) 90.

[16] P. D. Juhl, *Interpretation: An Essay in the Philosophy of Literary Criticism* (Princeton, N.J.: Princeton University Press, 1980) 149.

[17] A particularly poignant example of "feeling a connection to one's text" is Derrida. If any philosopher is aware of the logic of textuality – that writing disconnects a text from its author so that the text can "mean" even in the author's absence – it is he. But note that he accuses John Searle of having "avoided reading *me* and trying to understand."

But that is only *part* of the equation. For such is *not* my only relation with an other, nor is it even necessarily the most *important* relation. As a performer, I have a responsibility (perhaps even an equal responsibility) to those with whom I perform. And I have a responsibility to those who listen. Both of these relationships must *also* be taken seriously. Yet, even this formulation is not complex enough. For, if present performances have an effect on future performances (and it would be hard to argue the contrary, especially in the age of the CD), then I as performer have a responsibility to future listeners – and even future composers (who are also future listeners). The performance that I present in the present has a real effect on both performances and compositions in the future. I may not know what that effect will be. But I can be sure that there will be some such effect. *If* we can argue *environmentally* that we have some responsibility to those who come after us, *then* it seems obvious that we likewise have some *musical* responsibility to future generations. For music of today will undoubtedly be some part of the environment of tomorrow. No doubt, someone might object at this point that *musical* responsibility is hardly as important as *environmental* responsibility. But, even if we grant that point (and it may well be worth arguing), clearly music is not simply *unimportant*. And so my responsibility doesn't simply disappear.

But, if am right about these various responsibilities, then performers are faced with a remarkable challenge. And it may be impossible to do equal justice to each of these others. The problem is no less difficult for the composer. For, if the composer takes seriously a commitment to her art, to those who perform her music, and to those listen, the composer is faced

Derrida does not say "my text" but "me." See Jacques Derrida, *Limited Inc,* trans. Samuel Weber (Evanston, Ill.: Northwestern University Press, 1988) 113.

with a delicate balancing act – one that has no easy "solutions" and also must constantly be in flux in response to the given situation.

There is, of course, an easy way to solve this problem on the part of the composer. One can choose to compose "for the sake of art" or for one's self and immediate friends. The latter is the choice of Milton Babbitt, who freely acknowledges that his compositions can be appreciated by only a small group of musical *cognoscente* and refers to himself as a "vanity" composer.[18] Rose Rosengard Subotnik perfectly describes this sort of mentality when she says; "Ideally, today, the best composers write totally for themselves, without significant regard for audience or even performer."[19] Of course, I would question whether it is really appropriate to call these the "best" composers. Perhaps we should instead term them the "most narcissistic" composers. Here it is hard to miss the desire for autonomy of the sort that Levinas criticizes.

An obvious alternative course is – as artists often put it – to "sell out" to the listening public, giving them whatever they want to hear. But, while composers – and, for that matter, performers – may have reasons for taking either of these courses, I take it that they represent a false dilemma. One need not choose between the demands of art and the demands of performers and listeners – or at least not *absolutely*. As should be clear, though, taking the dialogical character of music seriously is much more difficult – and inevitably results in some degree of compromise.

---

[18] See Babbitt's now infamous article "Who Cares if You Listen?" *High Fidelity* (February 1958), reprinted as "The Composer as Specialist," in *Esthetics Contemporary*, ed. Richard Kostelanetz (Buffalo, N.Y.: Prometheus, 1978) 280–7. "Who Cares If You Listen" was the title chosen by the editor of *High Fidelity*, whereas "The Composer as Specialist" was Babbitt's choice.

[19] Rose Rosengard Subotnik, *Developing Variations: Style and Ideology in Western Music* (Minneapolis: University of Minnesota Press, 1991) 250.

To recognize a responsibility to dialogical others limits my free-dom and autonomy. But compromise is the stuff of life – or at least the stuff of truly ethical life. Because when we attempt to do justice to all of those we encounter, we are constantly faced with a juggling act.

As an example of someone who attempts to take this balance seriously, it is encouraging to hear the respected composer David Del Tredici say:

> Composers now are beginning to realize that if a piece excites an audience, *that doesn't mean it's terrible.* For my generation, it is considered vulgar to have an audience really, *really* like a piece on first hearing. But why are we writing music except to move people and to be expressive?[20]

Indeed, why can't music be both good and moving? Although the assumption has long been that truly "great" composers were never appreciated in their lifetime, the historical reality has been quite the opposite. Clearly, it is not impossible to find ways of "being true to one's art" and taking the others of the musical dialogue seriously. But there is no question that it is much more difficult. Ethical choices always are.

Perhaps there is a way of conceiving this relationship and its responsibilities that can make it less intimidating. If we are all partners in dialogue – none of whom can profess any absolute priority over any others – then the task of each participant is a dialogical task, one that is defined by that dialogue. If we are each participants, then none of us has the responsibility of con-trolling that dialogue – or even the *ability* to control it. Instead, we are simply members who attempt to respond to one another with respect. While that participation clearly calls for responsi-bility to the dialogical others, it likewise puts that responsibility

---

[20] Quoted in John Rockwell, *All American Music: Composition in the Late Twentieth Century* (New York: Knopf, 1983) 83.

into perspective. If I cannot control the dialogue, then I can only be expected to contribute to the best of my ability. And the same goes for all other participants.

Naturally, there are different ways in which this dialogue takes place. In a small group (such as a string quartet), there is a good degree of room for a genuine dialogue among all of the participants. This is even more the case in a small jazz group. Dave Brubeck has gone so far as to argue that "jazz is about the only form of art existing today in which there is freedom of the individual without the loss of group contact."[21] But that qualifier "about" may not be enough. Certainly, Brubeck is right in claiming that jazz provides a fine example of how it is possible for a group to allow for the existence of individual voices *and* still retain its group identity. What jazz demonstrates is that doing music *together* need not have the result of suppressing the individual. But, if what I have been arguing all along is correct, then this quality is not unique to jazz, even though the improvisation found in jazz may be a particularly good example of it. As should be clear, the larger the musical group, the more there is a need for a kind of mutual subordination of individual voices (figuratively and perhaps literally). But that subordination can be one that we *choose*. Whether a symphonic orchestra, a choir, or a jazz big band, such groups require a different kind of dialogue, one in which the members voluntarily give up some (and perhaps *much*) control of their voices to the conductor, who in effect turns them into a unified voice. But that is not to say that there is no dialogue in such cases; it is just that its dynamics have changed.

---

[21] Joachim E. Berendt, *The Jazz Book: From Ragtime to Fusion and Beyond*, rev ed., trans. H. and B. Bredigkeit with Dan Morgenstern and Tim Nevill (Westport, Conn.: Lawrence Hill, 1992) 161–2.

Music can provide an intense communal experience. But it doesn't always do so. Much listening to music today would seem to be in an individualistic context, partly because technology has made it possible to listen to music anywhere, the Walkman being perhaps the most vivid symbol of this development. Yet, even listening to music by way of a Walkman is an experience that includes an other, in an analogous way to reading a text. However far the other is away from us, however much we are unaware of the other and think of our musical experience as "private," there is still a sense in which we are connected to others: to those who have made (or else are currently making, if it is a "live" performance) the music to which we are listening and the musical tradition to which they in turn are connected. As Kathleen Higgins (rightly) points out, "Most listeners experience music, even that which comes to them through earphones, as a kind of communication between themselves and other human beings."[22] Furthermore, there is certainly room for a wide variety of musical experiences. Music can be something that brings us *all* together, but it can also be something that a particular group cherishes as its own and so unites them as a community. "Wagnerians" often feel a sense of kinship with one another, but there is no reason why a given Wagnerian could not be united with others by, say, a common love of Celtic music or Broadway musicals.

But, if being musical with the other involves a respect for all parties involved, how might that be worked out practically? I think that one possible way of answering this question is through the conception of "translation." Of course, we need a conception of translation that goes beyond the simple categories of "fidelity" and "license."

[22] Kathleen Marie Higgins, *The Music of Our Lives* (Philadelphia: Temple University Press, 1991) 151.

Living Voices

When music "ceases to be alive," claims Roger Sessions, "we can say in the most real sense that it ceases to be music."[23] Since much of the practice not merely of classical music but of jazz, blues, and rock music involves the re-presentation of that which has been presented before, we do well to begin with the notion of the "classic."[24] On the one hand, the classic is something that endures. It remains through time, not unchanged but with a strong sense of continuing identity. On the other hand, in defining something as "classical" there is always the danger of effectively – even if unwittingly – estranging it from the sphere of everyday existence. Precisely this sort of suffocating "respect" for and hermetic sealing of the past was what Landowska considered to be highly dangerous for the life of early music: "Ancient music! How harmful it was to name it so! Elevated upon a pompous pedestal and removed from mankind, 'ancient' music has lost its own life. Why? Could it mean that it never was alive?"[25] While claiming to honor the music of the past, we effectively deal it a lethal blow.

In what sense was ancient music *ever* alive? Was it alive in a radically different way from its life of today? Or has its life all along been structurally the same? As we noted in Chapter 3, a crucial assumption that often operates behind the revival of early music is that playing music of the past is substantially different from playing music of the present. Whereas the latter is a living

---

[23] *The Musical Experience of Composer, Performer, Listener* 71.

[24] While the notion of "classic" rock may sound like an oxymoron to some, we have reached a stage in the performance tradition of rock music in which the term "classic" truly does apply. For instance, Bob Dylan's "Like a Rolling Stone" and the album on which it appears – *Highway 61 Revisited* – clearly count as "classics."

[25] *Landowska on Music* 408.

phenomenon (one that has always been alive and thus needs no resuscitation), the former must be brought to life. The difference, then, would seem to be between the act of prolonging versus the act of resuscitating life. Yet, is there truly an essential difference? In a far more fundamental way, the two turn out to be the same: for, given that music exists only at the moment it is brought to sound, the process of bringing music into being is essentially the same no matter what its age. Since music does not fully exist except when performed, its existence is never continuous – whether in the living present or the past that once was a living present. As a result, it is never a question of simply prolonging music's life – that is, of keeping it alive – *but always one of bringing it to life once again.* All performance is resuscitation.

So how is music brought to life? Such a question concerns not merely performance but the entire process through which music comes into being. We have seen that the creation of music resembles a kind of improvised conversation. Working from within a particular context, composers join the ongoing musical dialogue not only with past and present composers but also with those who bring their pieces to sound and those who listen. Composition, then, is never merely an echo nor an original: it is both and neither, something that escapes any simple opposition. From its very origin to its final end, the existence of a piece of music depends on a kind of improvisatory translation: the effect of the tradition on the composer, the development of musical ideas and fragments into less fragmented but still essentially fragmented "pieces," the inscription of those ideas by way of dots and squiggles, the transformation of dots and squiggles into an acoustical existence, and the hearing that takes those moments of sound and blends them together to form a coherent whole. Of all of these sorts of translations, none is more important than the others. *All* are necessary for making music.

Were we to conceive of the activity of music making primarily in terms of "reproduction," then the binary opposition of "fidelity" and "license" might make sense (although, even in that case, it presents significant problems). But, having defined music making as essentially improvisational, that opposition is too simple, and also fails to describe the musical dialogue adequately. Note that *both* "fidelity" *and* "license" can be ways of *not* taking responsibility. Not only is it the case that as a performer my duties go beyond being *merely* faithful to the score (since my performance essentially supplements the score) but also attempts at "pure faithfulness" can be a way of avoiding taking any responsibility.

On the one hand, if my translation, whether musical or literary, claims to be merely "faithful" – neither more nor less – then I am in effect claiming to take no responsibility for what is being said nor how it is being said. In effect, I wash my hands of the matter, merely acting as the composer's "middleman." Such is precisely the strategy of the bureaucrat who claims to be merely enforcing the law. While someone operating in this way is likely to see himself as being "responsible," it is not an example of a willingness to take responsibility but actually an instance of *unwillingness*. On the other hand, while it is obvious that "license" can be irresponsible, in another sense license *can* be a way of taking responsibility. It is only in realizing that translation allows and even *requires* me to act creatively that I am able to take responsibility for what I am doing. Even bureaucrats are never simply "following the law," for every act of "following the law" requires interpretation of that law. However helpful and specific a law may be, it is always too general. We have seen that "scores" are always riddled with "places of indeterminacy" and, likewise, laws are never determinate enough. But this problem of generality does not merely apply to scores. Even performance traditions are not – in and of themselves – sufficient to guide the performer on how to act. Certainly, the combination of score and performance practice prove helpful guides. Yet, a performance requires not just one but multiple decisions on the part of the performer.

Kant's comments on genius illuminate what it means to take responsibility and why it is crucial to performance. As we have seen, Kant claims that what the genius creates "is meant not to be imitated, but to be followed by another genius." And the reason he gives here is crucial: for *"in mere imitation the element of genius in the work – what constitutes its spirit – would be lost."*[26] The goal of the musical translator must be neither pure imitation – which would result in death – nor pure innovation – which would result in distortion (and lack of respect). Instead, the goal must be a kind of continual *re*-creation (and note that I am using the term "creation" here in the carefully delimited sense defined in Chapters 2 and 3). Of course, there is a danger in using the term "re-creation," for it might be taken to imply that we are somehow attempting to duplicate something that once was and that the result can be, at best, no more than a mere imitation. Instead, the creation that performance brings about is not merely a "re"-creation, but (in its own way) a kind of *original.*

Walter Benjamin speaks of the life of a translation as being a kind of "afterlife," which is distinguished from its "original" life because it involves a transformation: "For in its afterlife – which could not be called that if it were not a transformation and a renewal of something living – the original undergoes a change."[27] Thus, a text – say, Thomas Mann's *Der Tod in Venedig* – takes on a new life as *Death in Venice.* Even if we say "it's still the same book," it is not *merely* the same. Part of this is because translators always create something more specific and defined than the original.

[26] *Critique of Judgment* 187 [§49].
[27] Walter Benjamin, "The Task of the Translator," in *Illuminations*, ed. Hannah Arendt, trans. Harry Zohn (New York: Collins, 1968) 73.

But, when we consider the "translation" that takes place in performance, the situation becomes far more complicated. What the score presents us is no more than a trace of the other's presence. In order for the sign to become a *living* presence, it must be transformed. Yet, if performance is both necessary for the piece to exist and has an essentially improvisational structure, then the "life" of a piece of music is found only in and through the afterlife of improvisation. Translation is not secondary or derivative *but essential.* And, since it is impossible for performers to speak for the other without adding their own voice, the true life of the piece of music always already includes more than one voice. *Only* in the improvisational "translation" of performance can there be any genuine speech.

But, if translation brings about a transformation in structure, then what justifies Benjamin's belief in the possibility of translatability? For he claims that "a real translation is transparent; it does not cover the original, does not block its light, but allows the pure language, as though reinforced by its own medium, to shine upon the original all the more fully."[28] To what degree is the improvisatory structure of performance "transparent"? As long as we are thinking in terms of mere transmission, then a translation that involves a transformation is less transparent than opaque, something that instead blocks the original. Although performers (or at least most performers) truly do wish to allow the "piece" to shine through, what that means must be clarified.

First, if the score can be taken as a written expression of what the composer wishes to say musically, then bringing the score to sound always requires saying that which is not directly said. As Mahler freely acknowledged, "The best part of music is not found in the notes." To make the piece of music come alive, the guidelines of the score – and even of historically appropriate

[28] Ibid. 79.

performance practice – are only a beginning point, not an end. Umberto Eco speaks of the "open works" of composers such as Berio and Stockhausen as being like "components of a construction kit."[29] But, as we have seen in Chapter 3, all pieces are of this character. A score is like a construction kit that includes only certain parts, and not even all of the most basic ones: for much of what is necessary to bring these parts to sound stands outside of the piece. In order for the performance to "shine upon the original," then, it must bring that original to light precisely by bringing it *into being*. Despite this, I think Fred Mauk seriously misses the mark when he says that "the performer is the one who constructs his own 'work' from the notations that the composer has left." Even though the performer is truly part of the "construction," what results is neither exclusively the "property" of the composer *nor* the performer. Thus the choice that Mauk provides the performer – "resurrection" (by which he means something like "transmission" or "repetition") or "insurrection" – is simply a false dilemma.[30]

Second, the goal of the performance likewise has to do with the continued growth and development of the piece. Derrida points out that Benjamin uses both the terms "*überleben*" and "*fortleben*" interchangeably. Yet, they are not the same, even though both translate into English as "survive." *Überleben* is a kind of survival by means of rising above the vicissitudes of existence – much like Ingarden's idea of the "super" historicality of the musical work. Were the translator simply interested in (and also *able*) to bring the text back to life as if there had been no intervening

---

[29] Umberto Eco, "The Poetics of the Open Work," in *The Open Work*, trans. Anna Cancogni (Cambridge, Mass.: Harvard University Press, 1989) 4.

[30] The choice that Fred Mauk makes is clear from his claim that "the only good composer is a dead composer." See his "Resurrection and Insurrection: Conflicting Metaphors for Musical Performance," *Journal of Aesthetics and Art Criticism* 45 (1986) 143.

history – as an ideal object that had risen above history and remained "pure" – then translation would be simply a matter of *überleben*. Note that the term for translation in German is *Übersetzung*, which literally means "taking over" or "bringing across." The idea is that there is an abyss separating the original text and the new audience, so that an *Übersetzung* spans that abyss and – in effect – closes the gap. Yet, that view of translation assumes not only that the original has remained "unchanged" but also that the intervening history can both be separated from the "original" and has no value in and of itself. Thus, on Derrida's account, the translator's job is not to "reproduce, represent, nor copy the original." Instead, "the translator must assure the survival, *which is to say the growth,* of the original. . . . This process – transforming the original as well as the translation – is the translation contract between the original and the translating text."[31] Given that a piece of music is a living entity, then its life must be characterized by an ongoing maturation process. Understandably, Derrida elsewhere suggests that "translation" might better be termed "transformation."[32]

How might we conceive this "transformation"? I think Derrida's own interpretation provides a guide. Geoffrey Bennington describes Derrida's way of reading texts as follows:

One can imagine Derrida as very modest, entirely occupied by reading and re-reading his predecessors with minute attention, determined to spend the time it takes over the slightest detail, the slightest comma, guardian of the letter of the old texts, putting nothing forward that he has not already found written by an other, scarcely our contemporary – and this is true. But, one can also imagine him, on the contrary, as immodesty

[31] "Roundtable on Translation," in *The Ear of the Other*, ed. Christie V. McDonald (New York: Schoken, 1985) 122.
[32] Jacques Derrida, *Positions*, trans. Alan Bass (Chicago: University of Chicago Press, 1981) 20.

itself, forcing these same old texts to say something quite different from what they had always seemed to say . . . and this is not false.[33]

No doubt, my suggestion that Derrida's way of interpreting could be helpful in thinking about the improvisation necessary to keep music alive may strike some as highly counterintuitive. For deconstruction has been used to further all sorts of projects, from the silly to the truly destructive. But "deconstruction" is actually a translation of Heidegger's notion of *destruktion* (destruction) and Husserl's notion of *Abbau* (literally, "unbuilding"). Heidegger introduces the idea of *destruktion* in order to open up the past and help us remember (or recover) that which the past has covered over. Heidegger points out that the history of philosophy is characterized by both preservation *and* forgetfulness. Thus, "destruction" is "a critical process in which the traditional concepts, which at first must necessarily be employed, are deconstructed down to the sources from which they were drawn."[34] So deconstruction – at least in the sense I am using here – is the attempt to return to original sources and to think about them anew.

Bennington claims that Derrida models for us *both* a kind of scrupulous *Werktreue* and interpretation that goes beyond simply fidelity. Regarding the first, note that Derrida has clearly emphasized the need for scrupulous interpretation. In the very paragraph above the one in which he makes the now infamous assertion "there is nothing outside of the text," he speaks of the need for a "doubling commentary" of a text with "all the instruments of traditional criticism" to serve as an "indispensable guardrail" to protect the text. Otherwise, interpretation "would

[33] Geoffrey Bennington and Jacques Derrida, *Jacques Derrida* (Chicago: University of Chicago Press, 1993) 6–7.
[34] Martin Heidegger, *The Basic Problems of Phenomenology*, trans. Albert Hofstadter (Bloomington: Indiana University Press, 1982) 23.

risk developing in any direction at all and authorize itself to say almost anything."[35] Yet, Derrida immediately goes on to point out that "this indispensable guardrail has always only *protected*, it never *opened*, a reading." *Neither* of these alternatives – at least taken to their logical extremes – would be desirable. On the one hand, the more one strives for a one-to-one correlation between interpretation and original text, the more the interpretation threatens to *become* the original text. On the other hand, the more one strives to be "creative" in interpretation, the further away from the original text one goes. The logical extreme, of course, is that the interpretation is no longer even connected to the original. Simply to remain an "interpretation" *of* something, the interpreter must hover between these two extremes.

It is this ability to work *between* these two modes – rather than choosing one over the other – that characterizes truly responsible musical improvisation. Often the best performances result when utmost scrutiny is paid to the slightest details *and* those details are given bold, innovative interpretations. Remarkably, Derrida and Harnoncourt turn out to be soulmates. No one would question that Harnoncourt's interpretations are driven by musical scrupulosity, as are those by many early music performers. But, in saying that "the familiar *St. Matthew Passion* revealed itself as an exciting *new* work,"Harnoncourt gives us a perfect example of this blend of scrupulosity and innovation. Thus, he is perfectly accurate when he writes: "What we accomplished was not the revival of an historical sound, not a museum-like restoration of sounds belonging to the past. *It was a modern performance, an interpretation thoroughly grounded in the 20th century.*"[36] Indeed, as we saw in Chapter 3, early music performers give us example after

---

[35] Jacques Derrida, *Of Grammatology*, corrected ed., trans. Gayatri Chakravorty Spivak (Baltimore: Johns Hopkins University Press, 1998) 158.

[36] *The Musical Dialogue* 73–4 (my italics).

example of this desire to be faithful (however defined) that ends up producing something delightfully new.

The Responsibility of Stewardship

While the fact that performance is essentially improvisatory (or "transformative") might seem to free the performer from restrictions, it actually does precisely the opposite. For it means that the performer has a tremendous responsibility, one that is far greater and more complex than one conceived in terms of simple transmission or reproduction or "fidelity." The performer, just like the translator, is essentially the inheritor of a gift – something bequeathed, unearned, and unowned.[37] As gift, it is something over which the performer does not have mastery or control. Moreover, it is not merely the piece of music that is bequeathed but, rather, the whole tradition to which that piece belongs and in which the performer and listener *merely* take part. Of course, such is the same for the composer: if composition can be described as a kind of improvisation on the work of other composers – indeed, on the entire tradition – then composers are likewise inheritors of a gift (and that in addition to the gift that we would see as the ability to compose). Thus, we have a responsibility to this gift that has been given to us. It is not *ours* in the sense of belonging to us or having been founded by us or being something that we can treat as we please. Rather, we are stewards of that with which we have been entrusted. That responsibility can be parsed out, variously, as responsibility to the giver

---

[37] In speaking of "the gift" here, I have in mind the discussion between Jacques Derrida and Jean-Luc Marion. See, for example, Jacques Derrida, *Given Time I: Counterfeit Money*, trans. Peggy Kamuf (Chicago: University of Chicago Press, 1992) and Jean-Luc Marion, *Etant donné: Essai d'une phénoménologie de la donation* (Paris: Presses Universitaires de France, 1997).

of the gift, to the gift itself, and to the fact that the gift has not merely been given to me. From my own perspective, all three of those aspects create my responsibility.

But, as we have seen, the complication that faces us as stewards is that this gift cannot be "kept" in the sense of being preserved. To do so would be like the steward in the Gospels who attempts to "preserve" the talent given him by way of burying it in the ground, an act that denotes not reverence but disregard. True, such an act keeps the talent "safe." But that talent is in no way allowed to develop and grow. Moreover, it is an act of *evasion*, for such a steward is, in effect, unwilling to take any real responsibility for what he has been given. Real preservation, instead, can be seen only in terms of both allowing that which one is given to grow and the nurturing that goes along with this preservation. To be a responsible steward is to improvise on that which one is given. It is to bring about a genuine *improvement*, in the senses we noted earlier. Precisely this goal of growth is what makes preservation so difficult, for the twin responsibility of tending and cultivating as well as allowing enough room for something to develop requires much more of us than the passive act of mere storage. It is the same dilemma (which is truly a dilemma, not something that can be resolved, not something for which there is anything like a "solution") that faces parents, who both want to allow their children enough room to grow and also want to protect them.

The challenge facing the performer is that of speaking both in the name of others – the composer, performers of the past, and the whole tradition in which one lives – and in one's own name, as well as *to* those who listen. It is an act that may or may not be successful. Performing and listening require developing an ability to listen to what the composer is saying and to let that voice be heard. And it can best be heard (and we can even go so far as to say that it can *only* be heard) in not being merely repeated. For mere repetition usually does not compel us to *listen*. The balance that one seeks – a balance that is probably never quite successful – is that of allowing the voice of the other to speak, without it swallowing up one's own voice. There is no golden mean here, for the balance is itself constantly changing and there are different ways of getting it right (as well as getting it wrong).

So what does all of this mean for the future of musical dialogue? One important need is that of overcoming the strict dichotomy between composer and performer so that we can see them both as essential to the improvisation process of making music. Undoubtedly, such self-proclaimed rebels as Boulez or John Cage or Max Neuhaus have played a part in paving the way for this way of thinking, for Cage's emphasis on experimentation has been a significant step in calling into question the work concept. But even more important has been the early music movement. For, despite whatever its practitioners have *said*, it has helped open (or, rather, *re*open) the door for improvisation. It has encouraged performers not to play the tired, written cadenzas for Baroque pieces but to create their own. Could that spirit of improvisation spill out more broadly into performance practice, perhaps even to ones that traditionally have been opposed to improvisation? Of course, jazz, blues, and many varieties of what is usually called "world music" provide us with living, vibrant examples of the kind of dialogue in which each member is important and has a voice. And their influence on the discourse of classical music is growing.

Just as important have been composers such as Philip Glass and performers such as Nigel Kennedy, the Kronos Quartet, and even Yo-Yo Ma. For they have done precisely what Kant suggests a great composer ought to do: improvise on the rules that govern musical practice. Glass has created an eclectic style that defies any precise definition. The Kronos Quartet presents concerts that include classical music but only as one item among others, such as jazz or world music. And Yo-Yo Ma's recent Silk Road Project at Carnegie Hall brings together composers from such diverse countries as Azerbaijan, China, Iran, Mongolia, and Uzbekistan.

Not only do Kennedy's concerts include a wide sampling of music, it is the *way* he puts that sampling together that proves important conceptually. For Kennedy does not present "works" but simply *music*. He has no qualms about playing a movement from a string quartet by, say, Fritz Kreisler (perhaps the first but just as likely the third or fourth), followed by a tune of Miles Davis; and then perhaps returning to another movement of that same string quartet, or something else all together. Similarly, the Kronos Quartet has shown us that Monk's "Round Midnight" can be improvised for a string quartet. We may be tempted to call this sort of performance practice "postmodern." But, in reality, this eclectic kind of programming characterized performances of the nineteenth century, and before. Pieces of music were treated precisely as "pieces" that could be put together and improvised upon in many ways to form a whole. Or, perhaps, it would be more accurate to say that there was no feeling of necessity that the result *had to be* a "whole." In performances of Kennedy and the Kronos Quartet there is no sense that one is hearing autonomous works, nor that one is hearing rock or blues or jazz or classical music. Instead, one just hears music.

"Let us return to old times," Verdi admonished, "and that will be progress." Earlier, we noted that there were two basic conceptions of music that flourished in the nineteenth century. On the one hand, Rossini considered his pieces of music to have a changing identity that was closely connected to their incarnations in performance and, as a result, his operas were treated as texts on which the performers improvised. On the other hand, it was Beethoven who demanded that his pieces be taken as "works" that had certain and inviolable boundaries. Theoretically, it was Beethoven's conception that has become the dominant one in the past two centuries. But, while this theory of the musical work has had a decisive impact upon musical practice, in a far more profound sense Rossini's view still more closely resembles the way in which a piece of music actually exists – even in the case in which performers are guided by the ideal of *Werktreue*. Music does not survive in the sense of *überleben*. It lives not "above and beyond" but, rather, *within* the musical dialogue.

Surprisingly enough, Stravinsky actually gives us an important clue as to what the musical dialogue really is. He claims that composers in effect invite the listener to be a partner "in the game initiated by the creator." He goes on to say that their relationship is "nothing less, nothing more" than a partnership.[38] But the piece of the puzzle that Stravinsky misses is that even the composer is merely an invited participant – one who is likewise only a partner in that game. That game is defined neither by the composer nor by the performer nor by the listener. It is a game that has a long history, a performance practice that has been preserved and handed down over the years. That game belongs to all of its participants, and none of them can claim priority. For the game – the very performance tradition of music making itself – is a gift that none of them own and no one player can control. It belongs to all of them and none of them.

Nothing more, nothing less.

[38] *Poetics of Music* 137.

Index

Adorno, Theodor, xiii, 137
Alperson, Philip, 143
aporia, 111–12
Aristotle, 137
Arnold, Malcolm, 43n22
arrangements, 10, 28, 30, 31, 156
authenticity movement (*see* early
    music)
autonomy, artistic, 164–6, 174

Babbitt, Milton, 174
Bach, J. S.
    composing practice, 21–2, 46,
      47, 57, 103, 105, 109, 119
    and improvisation, 20, 55, 56
    performance of his works, 98,
      100, 103, 105, 106, 109,
      111, 114, 116, 120
    St. Matthew Passion, 98–9, 106,
      111, 118, 119, 121–2, 129,
      152, 161, 169, 186

Baron von . . ., 36
Baroque music, 19–22, 27, 83,
    90
Bartók, Béla, 50
Basie, Count, 145
Baugh, Bruce, 165n3
Beardsley, Monroe, 66, 95–6,
    160
Beatles, the, 43
Beethoven, Ludwig van
    composing practice, 36–7, 53,
      59–61, 63–5, 119
    conception of musical
      "works," 16–18, 190
    Fifth Symphony, 11, 59–60,
      64–5, 116
    Hammerklavier Sonata, 74–5,
      93–4, 157
    and improvisation, 55
    intentions of, 71–2, 81
    Leonore Overtures, 61

Index

Index

Index

Index

defined, 23–4

and improvement, 32, 149–54

and interpretation, 143–6

and performance, 30–1, 82–5, 94, 119

as required, 26–7, 83–4

improvisus, 24, 32

inspiration, 35–6, 48, 53

intentionality, 34–5

intentions

of composers (or authors), xii, 11, 34–35, 70–5, 86–90, 104–10, 129, 160

letter versus spirit, 104–8

of listeners, 115–18

interpretation, 24–5, 143–6

Irrelevanzsphäre, 85–9

Ives, Charles, 158n44

Jackson, Roland, 49n32

James, William, 36

Josquin des Prez, 46

Juhl, P. D., 172

Kant, Immanuel

on genius, 36, 37–9, 50–2, 133, 138, 164–5, 181

on taste, 50–2

Karajan, Herbert von, 90

Kennedy, Nigel, 189–90

Kerman, Joseph, 113

Kern, Jerome, 161

Kierkegaard, Søren, 121, 165

Kivy, Peter, 39, 45, 56–7, 165n3, 172n14

Konrad, Ulrich, 59

Krausz, Michael, 82n10, 88n20

Kreisler, Fritz, 190

Kronos Quartet, 139n21, 189–90

Landowska, Wanda, 105, 106, 145, 178

Langer, Suzanne, 55–6

Le Huray, Peter, 81n6

Leonardo da Vinci, 113

Levinas, Emmanuel, 164–7, 174

Levin, Robert, 65

Levinson, Jerrold, 5, 10, 37, 39, 40, 42–3, 108

Lincoln Center Jazz Orchestra, 14

Listenius, Nicolai, 20n37

Liszt, Franz, 55, 166

Ma, Yo-yo, 189–90

MacIntyre, Alasdair, 41

McPartland, Marian, 136

Mahler, Gustav, 62–3, 182

Marion, Jean-Luc, 187n37

Marsalis, Wynton, 14

Mattheson, Johann, 46

Mauk, Fred, 183

Medieval music, 22, 103, 108

Mendelssohn, Felix, 98–9, 106, 111, 116, 119, 122, 129, 145, 152

Index

Merleau-Ponty, Maurice, 139n22, 154
metronome markings, 89–90
Meyer, Leonard, 50
Monk, Thelonious, 153, 190
Mozart, Wolfgang Amadeus
    composing practice, 29, 36–7, 39, 47–8, 50n34, 52–3, 57–9
    and improvisation, 55
    and musical conventions, 29, 47–8, 50
    performance of his music, 83–4, 92
    and restoration, 106
    scores of, 53, 101–2
Muffat, Georg, 46

Neuhaus, Max, 189
Newton, Isaac, 39
Nietzsche, Friedrich, 115, 155

opera buffa, 29, 47

Paganini, Niccolò, 166
Parker, Charlie, 48, 137, 140, 145
Pass, Joe, 145
Peirce, Charles Sanders, 8
performance
    and composition, ix–x, 13, 19–21, 83–5, 123–4
    and ideal objects, 7

and improvisation, 25–6, 30, 82–5, 94, 119
    limits of, 9–10, 93–6
    period instruments, 108–9
Pfitzner, Hans, 10
phenomenology, xi
piece, musical, 132–3, 148
plagiarism, 46, 60–1, 62
Platoff, John, 47
Platonism, musical, 6, 39, 129–30
Porter, Andrew, 92
practice, notion of, 41–42, 137, 140n24
prejudices, 120
Puccini, Giacomo, 42

Rembrandt van Rijn, 112
Renaissance music, 18, 22, 27, 83, 103, 108
representation (and presentation), 24, 133, 146
restoration
    ethical implications of, 122, 133
    of paintings, 112
    and sedimentation, 100, 120
    and unbroken tradition, 98–9, 178–9
    and "unrestoration," 119
resemblance, family, 159
Rivers, Sam, 134–5
Rochlitz, Friedrich, 36–7, 53
Rosen, Charles, 45–7, 157n43

Index

Index